Giulia Solaro della Margherita, Charles C. Pise

The Catholic Bride

or moral letters addressed to Julia, Daughter of Count Solaro della Margarita, on the occasion of her marriage with Count E. Demorri di Castelmagno

Giulia Solaro della Margherita, Charles C. Pise

The Catholic Bride
or moral letters addressed to Julia, Daughter of Count Solaro della Margarita, on the occasion of her marriage with Count E. Demorri di Castelmagno

ISBN/EAN: 9783741194092

Manufactured in Europe, USA, Canada, Australia, Japa

Cover: Foto ©ninafisch / pixelio.de

Manufactured and distributed by brebook publishing software (www.brebook.com)

Giulia Solaro della Margherita, Charles C. Pise

The Catholic Bride

THE CATHOLIC BRIDE;

OR

MORAL LETTERS

ADDRESSED TO

JULIA,

Daughter of Count Solaro della Margarita, on the Occasion of her Marriage with Count Eduardo Dencrri di Castelmagno.

Translated from the Italian by
CHARLES CONSTANTINE PISE, D. D.
Author of "Zenosius," &c. &c. &c.

BALTIMORE:
Published by John Murphy & Co.
182 Baltimore Street.
1868.

ENTERED, according to the Act of Congress, in the year one thousand eight hundred and forty-eight, by JOHN MURPHY, in the clerk's office of the District Court of Maryland.

DEDICATION
TO THE
Ladies of the Sacred Heart.

THE young Countess, to whom the following letters are addressed, was educated by the Ladies of your Society, at Turin. From them, she received that careful training, and those salutary lessons, which rendered her a model of piety, devotion, and all the gentle virtues. On this account, it seems to me but natural and proper that to you this little volume should be inscribed, as a testimony of respect and veneration, by

THE TRANSLATOR.

PREFACE.

THE volume containing the original letters, of which a translation is now offered to the public, was sent me, by the Very Reverend Father Grassi, from Rome,* accompanied by a kind suggestion that I should render them into our native tongue. By casting my eyes over a few pages, I perceived, at once, that they were a series of exquisite Epistles written by distinguished men, and among others, Silvio Pellico, and the Bishop of Asti, to a young and noble Bride, on the occasion of her nuptials. Although intended particularly for her, I saw, again, that they were fraught with excellent maxims, and wise counsels, from which any young Lady, and Parents, too, might derive no little profit. I felt that a translation would be adding another precious pearl to the sacred treasures of American Catholic Literature. As such I send it forth, with sentiments of gratitude to the venerable Father from whom it came, and of thankfulness for his suggestion, without which, perhaps, I should not have thought of performing a task so delightful to myself, and, I doubt not, so useful to thousands into whose hands it may chance to fall.

* Formerly President of Georgetown College, in the District of Columbia, afterwards Confessor to the Queen of Sardinia, and now filling a high office in the admirable Society to which he belongs.

CONTENTS.

LETTER I.—From the father to his daughter.....page 9

II.—From the mother to her daughter.......23

III.—From Mademoiselle A. Marovich......41

IV.—From Reverend Giuseppe Frasinetti....56

V.—From Silvio Pellico.................66

VI.—From the Bishop of Asti.............77

    MORAL REFLECTIONS.—From the same..79

VII.—From Reverend Filippo Storace......101

VIII.—From Reverend Dr. G. Ausidio........120

IX.—From Professor Carlo Ferreri to the Countess Solaro della Margarita.....151

    THE NUPTIAL BENEDICTION.........157

THE CATHOLIC BRIDE.

LETTER I.

FROM THE FATHER TO HIS DAUGHTER.

IT SEEMS but a day, beloved Julia, since your first cry broke upon my ear, and lo! you are now a bride. The precious charge which God entrusted to my care is transferred to another, on whom the duty of cultivating your heart, and ministering to your happiness, will, henceforth, devolve. Great is the joy of my bosom on this day; for he whose spouse you have become is a youth whose character forbids any inquietude, for the present, any apprehension for the future. And yet, I cannot but experience a sentiment of melancholy in parting with you. But how could it be otherwise? Were not you my first joy? Through you, your father and mother first began to taste the sweets of parental love: and the memory of you, floweret of the spring of life, mingles this moment of separation with feelings of sorrowful regret. Still my joy exceeds my grief, nay, even dispels it altogether, by the anticipation of your future felicity—felicity which depends, in a great measure, upon yourself—if you will not forget the instructions which you have received in your sacred retirement, where, for so many years, your heart has been formed to virtue by the example of your mother, a perfect model of mothers and wives.

It is to animate you to pursue the only way that leads to real happiness, that this series of letters is addressed to you: it will tend to show how you are to proceed in the new state of life to which heaven has called you. Let others compliment you with hymns and songs, and celebrate, in verse, the nuptial festivity. For my part, I do not regard you as created for this world, except that you may prepare yourself, in it, for the sublime reward which was promised you, when washed in the waters of baptism. You may, indeed, applaud the beautiful strains of the muse, but do not fix your heart on the prophecies of poets, or rely upon their flattering auguries, which are like flowers that blossom in the spring, but wither in the autumn. Rather let your thoughts rest upon those imperishable maxims of truth, which nothing can shake or destroy, and which survive, in their primeval integrity, all the changes and ruins of years. Look not upon your union as an ordinary act of life, which so many maidens view as a thing of indifference; but regard it as a solemn act of your vocation, and as a means, which God bestows, of arriving at eternal happiness.

Oh, Julia! my first born offspring! child of my tenderest love! think how brief is life, which now smiles so sweetly on you; how frail the flower of youth—how vain the scene around you! One thing alone is worthy of your esteem—one thing alone will fade not—VIRTUE! Beauty is short-lived; the grace of person fallacious; but virtue gives perfection to woman, and that for ever.

The world will seek to deceive and lead astray your tender heart. It will spread before your eyes the gorgeous festival, and present to your lips the cup of luxury: it will speak to you of its joys, as though they were real, and were never to have an end. It will deride the severe principles in which you have been educated, the counsels which have been inculcated, and the horror, with which you have been inspired, of any thing not conformable to the strictest sense of Christian morality. But heed it not; close your ears to its flattering language, as the deceitful song of the syren; stand firm to the principles which were dictated with quite another spirit, and for a very different end. The world desires to make you its own, not indeed for your welfare, but as another of its trophies; to add another ornament to its feasts, another victim of deceitful flattery, another example to be held up to incautious wives, whom it will long to deceive like yourself.

Who could enjoy more than your father the triumphs of this glorious day, and the great scene that now opens before your eyes, to which you have hitherto been kept a stranger, did he not know that all these rejoicings, these congratulations, these compliments, are but a dream, an illusion? Yes, God would condemn me, and I should offer violence to my own heart, were I, at this solemn moment, not to point out, with candor and parental solicitude, the way in which you should always walk, and which alone is worthy of a Christian lady. You are a gem, a treasure confided to my care by heaven for a definite time; but now, at the moment when you cease to be entirely mine, I desire to impress upon your mind all those sentiments which Rachel breathed into her daughter's heart when she became his spouse who, for having feared God, was worthy to be her consort. Hearken, then, to these few words; sacred are the words which the father utters to his daughter; and she will be blessed by God if she but hearken to them.

Your first duty, then, is to love the husband whom God has given you, and who is to be yours, as you are to be his, in an indissoluble bond, even unto death. For him you leave your parents, your sisters, and your brother. For him you bid adieu to the house in which you were ushered into the light of day. For him you should be prepared to abandon every thing—every thing but God. To him must God alone be preferred. By respecting the authority of your husband, by proving your affection for him, by being faithful to him, you will enjoy that peace of heart which of all blessings is, indeed, the greatest.

The world will persuade you to participate in its vanities, and be, as it were, a stranger in your own family, of which you should prove the purest ornament, and the most precious part. But remember that God requires of you the very contrary; that you should place your glory in your domestic affairs, and in a strict attention to the demands of your family. The world will offer you its plaudits, and shower upon you its brilliant encomiums, and invite you to indulge in its luxuries and pleasures, but let your noble heart aspire to other encomiums, ambition the eulogy for which the resolute woman was celebrated by the wisest of men and kings, in the book of Proverbs. He does not praise her passing beauty, nor her wonderful talents, nor her winning and graceful elegance of manner before men, nor the accomplishments with which she was adorned, and by which she could make hearts captive; but he praises her vigilance in her household concerns, the order with which she regulates her family, the attention which she pays to the interests of her house. According to the language of the world, it is a disgrace to the sex for a lady to apply herself to the needle and the "spindle." But different is the declaration of the Increated wisdom by the mouth of Solomon. When he says that the "valiant woman" did not disdain the "spindle," he uses the terms, so memorable and worthy of your meditation: "She hath put out her hand to strong things."* By strong things one might be led to suppose that he meant wonderful enterprises, renowned achievements, by which she obtained the admiration and glory of the world. But no; "her fingers," he adds, "have taken hold of the spindle." What important lessons are contained in these simple words, which confound the pride of human thought! But, before God, my beloved child, he is not reputed great or valiant, who acquires celebrity by noisy and dazzling deeds; but he is great and valiant who fulfils his duties in the sphere in which God's will has placed him, whether that be large or small, and

* Prov. chap. xxx, v. 19.

having fulfilled these, he achieves a triumph, and shall not fail to receive his crown.

Bear these things in mind, daughter of my heart, and by following this path, you will have no bitter regrets, when the last moment draws nigh. And after you shall have attained the fulness of years, as I trust, and shall yourself have become the mother of a numerous offspring, repeat these counsels to your children; tell them to live, as you have done, under the ægis of the fear of God. Your house will, thus, become a blessed home in the interior world, in which all your thoughts and sacred solicitudes will be centred.

Oh! thrice happy, my dearest Julia, if, surmounting the prejudices of this age, conquering human respect, the fatal enemy of every virtue, which stifles its germ in the loveliest hearts, you will prove that you prefer, to the splendor and flattery of the world, that solid and only substantial eulogy which a Christian bride should seek after: "Her children rose up and called her blessed; her husband, and he praised her. Many daughters have gathered together riches; thou hast surpassed them all."* If it appear difficult to arrive at this goal, you will not find it so, provided you gird yourself with courage; not trusting, however, in your own weak energies, but in the all-powerful assistance of God. He who created you for himself, and who now gives you a generous companion to be your guide and comfort in your career through life, will support you with his grace, and enable you to overcome all obstacles, and to triumph over the infirmities of nature.

I might add more, my daughter, were I not unwilling to exceed the limits of a letter; or were there not others to follow,

* Idem. vv. 23, 29.

in a strain of deeper wisdom, and a style of greater elegance, which will be presented to your young mind, not like a bouquet of perishable roses, but of immortal flowers of virtue. I hand them to you; preserve them and profit by them, as the pledge of that paternal affection, the strength of which neither you nor any other can conceive, but which is known to God alone. Yes, my child, most precious gift of heaven, joy of my heart, at this moment when I am to separate from you, I feel how dear this gift has been to me, and the sacrifice I am making. Nevertheless, I deem myself happy, if your consort will be able, in future years, to say that you have been, likewise, a gift to him, and, confiding his heart in yours, he may bless the bride whom he has received from my hands, and from God.

Oh! what a jubilee was it for my house, I repeat it. on that day that gave you birth! It seems a dream, indeed. The time has come when this jubilee is to be taken into another family. Go, then, awaken it within those halls, which are already adorned for your festival; enter them as the young Sarah entered into the house of Tobias; carry thither light and peace. My vows accompany you, and these my vows carry with them the most abundant paternal benedictions. I pray the Almighty Giver of all good gifts to ratify them in heaven, and to receive them with that plenitude of favor, which I shall never cease to implore for you, with all the affection of my heart.

Adieu, dear child, be happy; heed not the tear which, at the moment of parting, steals from the eyes of your parents. It is blended with smiles. Our hearts are filled with gratitude to that good God who gave you to us, and who comforts you now with the hope of a blessed future. ' This must be the portion of a woman who "loves her husband, takes care of the family, governs the house, and behaves herself irreprehensibly."*

Your most affectionate father,
                    CLEMENTE.
TURIN, *August* 4th, 1845.

* Tobias, chap. x, v. 13.

FROM THE MOTHER TO HER DAUGHTER

Beloved Julia,

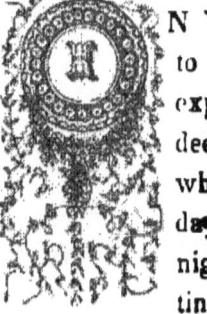

IN VAIN should I attempt to find words adequate to express the affections, the deep and lively emotions, which I experience, as the day of your nuptials draws nigh, a day on which, quitting your paternal home, you will leave behind you sweet and tender reminiscences. In them I now console myself: and, in order to perpetuate the memory of them, while I commit them to writing, on the wings of airy thought I am transported back to the banks of the Manzanares, in the capital of the "Catholic kingdom," where you first saw the light of this passing world, and where my longing wish was accomplished to become a mother. Oh with what transport of joy, and thanksgiving to God, did I press you to my bosom, so lovely and precious a gift of heaven! But even then there was a mixture of uneasiness with my bliss; your person, indeed, was beautiful, but your soul was stained with the sin of our first parents; and while I could call you my child, I could not style you the child of God. Anxiously did I watch the entire night which preceded your regeneration: and I trembled until the instant when you were carried to the sacred font, where from the hands of the illustrious prelate*

* Monsignor Giustiniani, archbishop of Tyre, nuncio of his Holiness near his Catholic majesty: since cardinal of the holy Roman church.

who was afterwards honored with the sacred purple, you received the sacrament of baptism, and were brought back, an angel, to my arms. Who can tell the throbbings of my heart, and how beautiful faith made you to my eyes. A sister of the angels, a daughter of the Most High, destined to the bright spheres of paradise. I know not what hymn of gratitude and praise I entoned; but this I know, that hugging you to my heart, and raising on high my feeble arms, I offered you wholly to Him who gave you to me, and under his protection I placed you, imploring him to shower upon your head his copious benedictions, which have accompanied you thus far, and will, I cannot doubt, continue with you during your existence below.

The day of your baptism had not reached its meridian, before, disregarding my weakness, I nourished at the fountain of my own breasts that life which it had pleased God to bestow upon you: and I passed, in the capacity of your nurse, the first sixteen months of your infancy. Sweet did my anxieties, cares, and sleepless nights appear; and sweet is the task at present, though ignorant of the language of the muses, to preserve their recollection.

Meanwhile, new consolations were in store for me, whilst trying to impress on your infant mind the sublime truths of religion: the ancient story of our progenitors, the first notions most worthy and most necessary to be known; on which, forgetful of your natural vivacity, you hung as they dropt from my lips. You may, perhaps, yourself remember the tears I shed when, having attained your seventh year, we abandoned the land of your birth. That was a foreign land to me; but there, for the first time did you call me mother!

The long journey which brought us back to my country was full of anxiety: I feared it might have proved prejudicial to your tender age; but heaven preserved you, and here, in Turin, you have continued to be the object of my most pleasing cares. As you advanced in years, your mother's heart trembled for your life, for I beheld you ill and languid. But again heaven watched over your safety: we invoked its protection, and your health was restored, and you were rendered still more precious, because I had feared we should lose you. As years increased, my solicitude for your welfare and happiness increased in proportion; and convinced that these blessings are to be found in innocence alone, I shuddered at the snares of the perverse and deceitful world. I poured out a sea of tears. I shut you up in the asylum of the Ladies of the Sacred Heart of the Redeemer, caring nothing for my sacrifice when your interest and felicity were at stake. Within the precincts of those sacred retreats you passed the joyous days of childhood, ignorant of the wiles of the world, of its dangerous arts, and its poisonous delights. There you tasted the blessed sweets of virtue, of friendship: and admiring in your angelical guides the heroic sacrifices which they made for God's sake, you saw them never sad or dejected as they are reported by the world, but enjoying ineffable bliss, and anxious about nothing save the eternal recompense with which they are destined to be crowned.

With a heart glowing with religion and virtue you returned to your paternal roof rejoicing. And oh! with what rapture were you received! I said from that moment you were to be your mother's companion. .... But I was mistaken. Whilst enjoying, with me, the sacred tranquillity of nome, God was preparing a blessed union for you. Already are you affianced, and after a few more days you shall become a wife.

At this crisis, my mind is agitated by a thousand emotions of grief and of joy, and I am almost unable to utter my sentiments. But no; I must speak, and reason with you now, my darling daughter, and remind you of many a conversation which we have often prolonged till midnight; in which your ingenuous mind seemed rapt, and your tender heart was filled with interest. Then did I urge upon you—young and inexperienced maid—the most salutary reflections on the necessity of education, the priceless value of virtue, and the vanity of earthly things. Sometimes fixing our eyes on the starry firmament I essayed, but in vain, to give you an idea of the greatness, majesty, immensity, and omnipotence of Him who drew this universe out of nothing. I showed you the folly of the atheist, who rejects him, and the believer who does not serve him. I conjured you to invoke that heavenly Father, to love that eternal friend, to offer him the thoughts, affections, aspirations of your youthful heart. I entreated you to obey his precepts, not only those that require little sacrifice, but those also that are difficult to be fulfilled—to observe all, even at the cost of your life.

And of what did I not discourse, to teach you to love Him? Of his ineffable beauty, his admirable wisdom, his omnipotent power, and his infinite attributes: and if I could not succeed in speaking of them as I desired, it was because they are so incomprehensible and sublime, that the language of the Seraphim could not express them. I told you that he created you without any merit of yours, placed you in the hallowed pale of his church, gave you Christian parents,—and I related to you the virtues and qualities of your noble father. God favored you with a lively imagination to know him, a discerning mind to appreciate the excellent, the beautiful, the great, an ardent heart to love him, and a pious disposition to obey his law. Upon you, moreover, he lavished temporal blessings: for you the rich harvests covered the fields, beauteous flowers adorned the meadows, and to you were poured out, in abundant streams, the pellucid fountains of education. And now is given to you a husband, selected by the providence of God, from the eternal years, a youth worthy the beneficent giver, by his transcendent qualities and his noble soul. Oh, my dearest daughter! such multiplied favors call for your deepest gratitude. I know you have promised eternal fealty, and that promise will be inviolable. Is not God the perennial source of all good? Has he not in his hands the treasures of the earth? Can he not, at his pleasure, pour out upon the prevaricating children of Adam the vial of his wrath, or scatter, in profusion, his temporal blessings among his faithful servants? Consequently, even your own interest should induce you, my beloved Julia, to propitiate his favors by a life of devotion and faith. Oh foolish mortals! in your anxiety to procure riches, honors and happiness, how often do you not besiege the mansions of the great, who either will not or cannot grant what you demand! and you forget that duty by which you may be certain of obtaining, not vain and perishable wealth, and honors, and felicity, but an unspeakable and eternal "weight of glory."

Remember now those salutary considerations. Let not the sun beam in the bright sky of morning, or fade in the misty horizon of evening, without sending up the incense of prayer to his throne. Invoke him reverently in his temple, assist devoutly at the holy sacrifice, eagerly drink of the living waters of the sacraments, and let his divine word be sweeter to you than honey and the honey-comb. Look with abhorrence upon those who make a boast of insulting religion, ridiculing devotion, contemning the laws of God and of the church—laws which are not a heavy burden, but a yoke, light and sweet, of infinite love. If you continue faithful to my instructions, my prophecy shall certainly come to pass: more numerous than the stars of heaven, or than the sands of the sea, shall the blessings of the Omnipotent descend upon you, O my dearest daughter: and the favors already received will be nothing in comparison with those which are yet in store for the consolation of your future existence.

The pleasing subject of many a protracted discussion was She, who, mantled with the sun, crowned with stars, and treading on the moon, reigns the Sovereign of the empyrean. Often did you yourself love to speak of her to me, and often did you press to my lips her image which hung around your neck, declaring it to be dearer to you than gems or precious stones, and glorying in the august appellation of the child of Mary, a title which though common to every true believer, belonged to you by a more special claim, as it was your blessing to be enrolled in the pious "Congregation of the children of Mary." This was a cheering and delightful circumstance to me. For, I felt that if that benignant star would be propitious to you, he perils of life's tempestuous ocean would be safely encountered: I knew that to imitate an object so tenderly loved would be an easy and agreeable thing, as that virtue would appear the more lovely for having been practised by the immaculate Queen of heaven. And of what sublime virtues is she not an example? How brilliantly did sanctity shine in her? Mary showed that it does not consist, as some appear to imagine, merely in bending prostrate at the foot of the altar, in being clad in sackcloth, girt with chains, or shut up and secluded amid deserts and solitudes; but it is mild, cheerful, patient, social, intent on doing the will of the Most High, and in discharging, with inviolable fidelity, the duties of our state of life. If we contemplate Mary in her childhood, she is the model of incomparable innocence, incontaminate virginity, devoted to retirement and prayer. And when, by the divine decree, she was chosen to be made the spouse of Joseph, we see her humble, affectionate, and obedient to her holy consort. O you who, in your childish days, imitated her in her retirement under the shadow of the temple, and in the preservation of her spotless virtue, imitate her yet; happy if you walk in her blessed footsteps, by loving your husband, centering in him all the affections of your heart, and keeping for him the sweet accents of your lips. His happiness should form the object of your solicitudes; that should you procure him, no matter how great the sacrifice required. More sweet to him will you be, by sharing with him your joys; more dear, by dividing with him your troubles. Let your thoughts hold communion with his; encourage him to emulate the virtues of his ancestors, and exert his noble character in generous deeds; to prove his fidelity to the august prince who reigns, and be the zealous champion of his native land, and of the ancient faith. Honor him as your head. Forget not that the woman was created subject to man, that obedience is the first of your obligations, that every wish of his should be sacred to you, and even should you seek, as far as possible, to anticipate his wishes. Did I not know the character of your husband, I would prescribe a limit to this counsel; but no wish of his will ever be contrary to the sacred laws of religion. Honor his mother, dearest Julia, and by your innocent mirth relieve the mourning of her widowhood: divide with her your household cares, reverently listen to her advice, imitate her example, and let all who appertain to your husband, either by blood or dependence, be the objects of your incessant care.

But, if Mary was an intemerate spouse, she was a mother also, and the most blessed of mothers: the only one who, by an unheard of prodigy, knew how to unite the most glorious fecundity with the most immaculate virginity. And oh! the sublime examples of maternal love and maternal solicitude which she presents for our salutary instruction! If, at some future day, God should bestow on you the grace of becoming a mother, then will you remember the lessons which she, as such, imparts. The emotions of my soul, and my feeble health, prevent me from continuing. My pen seems wearied at the effort I have already made. But still, I have strength enough remaining to bid a tender adieu, to implore again for you the blessings of kind heaven, to express again my heartfelt hopes of the future, to conjure you never to be unmindful of the house of your parents, and to invoke upon your consort and yourself the copious blessings of heaven and of earth. Stretch out your hands to "strong things." By your industry your fields will become more productive, your vines more fruitful, your gardens more blooming, your affairs more prosperous. Take into your fingers the "needle and the spindle," shun idleness; let your lamp never be extinguished; let not the shadows of night interrupt your watchfulness. Thus your domestics shall not fear the heat of summer, nor the cold of winter. Succor and console the miserable, the needy, the forsaken. Let your tongue distil accents of sweetness and wisdom. And while "fine linen and purple are the covering" of your person, "strength and beauty" will be the clothing of your soul. In your love and inviolable fidelity your husband's heart will tranquilly and securely rest, and you will be to him the harbinger of every good, if he sees in your feeble sex a manly soul. May your offspring be numerous, and may they surround the hearth of your generous consort, as the vine clings, with its purple progeny, to the tree that supports its branches. May they be a source of consolation to the church to their native land, and to Him who will give them birth. Cultivate, with care, those tender plants, and let them call you blessed. May your days be long and happy on the earth, and when this mortal life shall be drawing to its close, may a gentle smile, even to the end, play upon your lips, and reveal to the standers-by, the contentment of your heart, for having, from your earliest youth, cherished in your soul this memorable maxim of the wise man: "favor is deceitful, and beauty is vain: the woman that feareth the Lord, she shall be praised."*

    Your most affectionate mother,
          CAROLINA.

TURIN, *August 9th*, 1845.

    * Proverbs xxxi, 30.

LETTER III.

FROM MADEMOISELLE ANNA MARIA MAROVICH.

My Dear young Countess,

WHENEVER I hear of a truly Christian lady, who is not called to pass her life in religious celibacy, entering, with the consent and benediction of her parents, on the matrimonial state, with a man of equal rank and merit, my soul exults with joy, and is filled with delightful hopes. This was the case of late, when your most excellent father kindly communicated to me the intelligence of your affiance: and if, ere this, I have not ex-

pressed my feelings to you, as I should have done, it was on account of indisposition under which I have been suffering during several days. My heart responds, with deep emotion, to the tidings: its aspirations are intense for your future happiness, and its prayers are fervent for heaven's blessings on you. Deem it not strange, that, because I have not embraced the marriage state myself, I should rejoice at the nuptials of another. I prefer—to speak the truth—virginity to matrimony: but while I love and honor virgins, as the most noble portion of the flock of Christ, I honor and respect the married; who, although in a less elevated and perfect state can, notwithstanding, with the divine assistance, punctually discharge their respective duties, render themselves meritorious in the church of God, by fulfilling a mission, and an apostleship, the more efficacious and useful, because of the greater force of their natural attractions.

Woman, we see from daily experience, can have a powerful influence over the heart of man; and, by her insinuating manners, can easily lead him on to good or evil. Eve, our common mother, has given a melancholy proof of this power: and her example is imitated by too many thoughtless girls, who seem to marry for no other purpose than to lead to perdition their husbands, and their children, with themselves. But a true wife, a Christian wife, will not exert her meek influence over her husband's heart, except to purify its defects, and fortify it in the practice of every virtue.

The unbelieving man, says the great apostle Paul, will be sanctified by the believing woman. And of this fact history will furnish innumerable instances. Not to speak of the Cecilias, the Monicas, and so many others who might be mentioned in testimony of this truth, I will relate a circumstance to which I myself can bear witness. A dear friend of mine was married to a gentleman who was irreproachable in every particular, except that he felt the greatest repugnance to the sacraments, of which, even at the Easter time, he would not participate. His pious wife mourned over his fatal negligence, for which she could not account, knowing him to be an upright and honest man. A thousand times did she represent to him the danger to which this negligence exposed him, but in vain. To her remonstrances he answered, it is true, with promises, which were never fulfilled. Meanwhile he loved his wife with all the intensity which her virtues deserved, and could not bear to be absent from her, even for a moment. She determined to avail herself of this devoted affection, and to lead her husband insensibly through it to that love which is the "one thing necessary." Profiting by the unhappiness he felt in being absent from her, "reflect," she one day said, "if it is so painful for you to be away from me so short a time, how will you be able to endure an eternal separation?" He fixed his earnest gaze on her, not immediately understanding the import of her language. "Yes," she resumed, "my beloved husband, I fear this may be the case, because while I endeavor, by obeying the commandments of the church, to save my soul, through the merits of our divine Redeemer, you continue to keep yourself from the sacraments, the channels of grace and life. And although in other respects, your conduct is that of a regular Christian, how can you hope to be saved, by the mere exterior profession, without the interior and practical influences of religion and faith? Will you run the risk of being separated from me for all eternity?" So deep was the impression made, by these words, on the mind of her husband, that, from that moment, he resolved to change his life. He began to approach the sacred tribunal of penance, and the holy table, anew; and so faithfully did he persevere, that it was easily seen how successfully the holy artifice of that good wife was blessed by the Lord, who brought him back, by his grace, to a sense of duty, and kindled, by means of a purely earthly and natural love, the heavenly and blessed fire of supernatural charity.

Your pious and enlightened parents have, I doubt not, selected for you a husband for whose conversion you will not have to labor. But I thought proper to relate this fact in order to make you see, more clearly, what a Christian wife may effect by her prayers and exhortations, and in what manner she can and should make use of the affection which her husband cherishes for her, to procure, if not his conversion, which may not be required, at any rate his greater sanctification. You may learn, besides, the object for which woman has been made: to be the companion of man, and to help him in his various wants on earth, and, above all, to aid him in obtaining the great end for which he has been created. Justly, therefore, does the church expect, and God require, the sanctification of the husband through the influence of the Christian wife. And oh! what a wrong is not inflicted upon both one and the other, by those foolish women, who, instead of cooperating as far as possible, in the attainment of that end, by their evil example, their derision of piety and good works, and their habitual dissipations of mind and body, keep themselves and their husbands at a greater distance than ever from it.

Nor is this the only mission entrusted, by Providence, to a truly Christian wife. Should you become a mother, a wider field will open to your glorious and gentle apostleship. God confides to the care and training of the mother the stainless souls of her innocent children, that she may preserve them pure and incontaminate. To her the church commits them, as the first cultivator of that virginal soil, which, in progress of years, will bring forth fruit, either good or bad, in conformity with the nature of that first-sown seed. Oh! what merit, then, will not that mother acquire before heaven and earth, who, from the tenderest years of her children, labors to impress upon their minds as upon soft wax, the seal of the evangelical maxims, and Christian doctrine! Infancy, precious infancy, God confides, in a special manner, to the direction of the mother: and yet too many mothers give over to the care of mercenary nurses their little ones, who stand, most particularly, in need of sacred attention. And who can tell how soon their tender hearts take in impressions which may never be eradicated. The virtuous sentiments impressed by a mother's love into her children's breasts, may, indeed, as they grow in years, be stifled and almost choked by the thorns of increasing passions, but there remains a vital germ which, at a more sober period, may shoot forth, and blossom, and bear the flowers and the fruits of virtue and faith.

Did not the short space of a letter forbid my dilating on this interesting topic, how much more might be added, and how many instances adduced, in confirmation of what I have said? You yourself are one. For, if you have grown up in virtue and devotion, if the fear and love of God have ever dwelt in your tender heart, you owe it all to the example and the religious education which you have received from your noble mother, who, together with her excellent husband, your magnanimous father, is a model of every Christian virtue. Imitate the example which your home has given you, and you will prove a wife according to God's own heart. Be careful, in the midst of the world, to shed around the sweet odor of Jesus Christ. Be docile and amiable to your husband, and towards his family, but be still more solicitous to please the heavenly spouse of your soul, who, indeed, permits you to participate in the innocent enjoyments of the world, but forbids your becoming a slave to its pomps and its vanities. Dress in a manner becoming your high rank, but, at the same time, bewail, with Esther, the necessity of so doing, and abhor every thing that does not tend to ornament the soul. Esteem not personal beauty, that short-lived flower, which often fades as it blooms, but stamp on your memory the maxim of the Holy Ghost: "the woman fearing God, she shall be praised!" Be solicitous to embellish your mind with solid and lasting ornaments, seeking to advance more and more in virtue, which, while it renders you beautiful and pleasing in the sight of heaven, gives a charm in the eyes of men, and especially of his to whom God unites you. The indispensable virtues of a wife are humility, obedience, meekness, condescension, modesty, chastity, prudence, activity, equanimity, patience, and, above all, love of God, of her husband, and of her neighbor, the source of every other virtue. Be attached to home, and be prudent in the liberty which is generally supposed to be allowed to married women. But be ready to go into society, when your husband wishes, or your social duties require it. Be not dazzled by the pomps and the vain splendor of the world; and do not seek delight in the pleasures which it offers to the young and gay. Solomon had seen and tasted all the delights and fascinations of the world, and he pronounced them all to be vanity and affliction of spirit. God alone can satisfy and render happy the human heart, which has been created only to love and enjoy Him. The treasures, enjoyments, and creatures of the earth may distract and please it for a moment, but they cannot satisfy its cravings, cannot give it peace. The disgust they leave behind attests their vanity. No pleasure on earth can be compared with that which is the fruit of heavenly peace; peace which none can imagine, save those who live in the fear and love of God. Ah! one only drop of that, which surpasses all understanding, is far more worth than every human consolation. That peace is not false nor transient; but real and enduring: for as long as we live virtuously and piously, it will abide with us, and, after death will follow us to the realms of bliss— such is the peace which the world cannot give!

Keep your heart and soul, as far as possible, fixed on God. Meditate, frequently, his infinite grandeur, and the eternal recompense which he has in store for those who love him and serve him faithfully on earth. Compare the pleasures of heaven with those of the world, and see how the latter vanish, like a shadow, before those of the former. By so doing, it will be an easy task, while living in the midst of the world, to preserve your fidelity to heaven, and be a good wife, an excellent mother, a wise and virtuous matron. Moreover, your pious example will animate others, will be pleasing to your husband, and render religion more endearing to him. Educate, with sedulous care, your children, and train them up as so many citizens of the heavenly Jerusalem. You will, thus, spread through your household, your friends, and the votaries of the world itself, the sweet fragrance of Christian virtues, and will convince all that to practise them is not as difficult as is generally supposed: for which, it is not necessary to fly to the desert, nor withdraw from the rank in society to which they have been called.

For myself—unworthy servant of the Lord—who am capable only of suggesting some salutary advice, to one who hardly needs it—I pray his goodness to accept what I have written in supplication for your future prosperity. Nor should I have had the courage to attempt this task, had not your most excellent father condescended to request it of me. Receive it, as the outpourings of a sincere heart, which desires your temporal and eternal welfare; and overlook the inelegance and plainness of my style. Do not forget me in your fervent prayers, and be assured, that you shall always have a place in mine. Persevere to the end, in the sweet and sacred love of God, in the peace of our blessed Redeemer, under the protection of Mary, his most holy mother, the model of a Christian wife: and believe me to be, with profound esteem, most noble countess, your devoted and obliged friend.

ANNA MARIA MAROVICH.

Venice, *July 19th,* 1845.

LETTER IV.

FROM THE PRIOR OF ST. SABINA.

Illustrious Countess:

BEHOLD the world is making a festival for you, now that you have reached the goal to which you have been destined. From this season, the tender flower of life opens to the sunbeams that sparkle with dew, inhales the fragrance of the balmy zephyrs, and seems to have no dread of the venom of insects, of the burning heat, or the pelting rain, or the destructive hail. That this joyous scene may last, is the prayer of a hundred maidens, your pure and gentle companions. Can this be but a vain enchantment? How delightful is the harmony made by a thousand plaudits, and the happy auguries of a thousand voices! Some proclaim the lustre of your ancestors, some the splendor of your family, some the qualities of your mind, some the beauty of your person: every where is homage paid, every where are gratulations offered: while the hand of your distinguished husband holds out a certain pledge of future happiness. Permit me, amid these festive offerings, to mingle the tribute of my congratulations: persuaded that the pæans of joy and eulogy that ring around you will not be able to silence the voice of sober and sage reflection. A wise woman, like yourself, enjoys the festival which the world will make on occasions like this: but she does not suffer her heart to be fascinated by its witchery. She tastes the goblet of con tentment, but still she knows, full well, that it is mixed with imperfection. She cherishes the flower of her youth, but does not forget how evanescent and frail it is. Wherefore she is moderate in her rejoicings, serene in mind, calm in heart. The new career of life that spreads before your eyes, seems, indeed, at first, all strewn with roses, but it is untried, and requires that you should tread it cautiously. You will not then, refuse to accept, with kindness, the reflections which occur to me, in the midst of the solemnities and gratulations of this joyous hour.

You are walking, it is true, on a path of roses: but remember it is a road and not a garden: and these flowers are not without thorns. When you enter into a garden, it is to amuse yourself, and you can walk, or stop, or sit, or return, at will: but when you have once entered upon your journey on the road of life, you must continue forward towards the destined goal, and no time can be spent in vain. That goal is proposed to all mortals alike, but is reached by various paths, and at the hour and moment predetermined by God —I mean eternal felicity. The pilgrim, on his way, is, sometimes, arrested by the attractive scene, but if he do not reach the inn in time, he bewails, at night, the hours lost by day. This admonition is suitable to a lady of your rank, surrounded by the fascinations of the world. You have, at your command, whatever you desire: the theatre, the ball, the brilliant saloon, and every amusement which the city or the villa can offer to a person of your elevated condition. And the world, which knows no other wisdom but pleasure, pleasure which it adores, to which it sacrifices every thing besides, invites, stimulates, and almost forces your young heart to yield to its influence, and consent to be a victim. But resist its syren violence: and be not induced to stop on your way to that destination, which is the only object of your journey through the vale of years.

No one is perfectly content below: whether his lot be cast among the common people, whether he glitter among the rich, or tower among the great, or reign among the sovereigns of the earth. Our end is not the fallacious happiness of the world, but the solid bliss of heaven: if we seek the former, we will lose the latter: for two contrary ends cannot be attained at the same time. But terrestrial happiness, as the world presents it to its deluded votaries, is opposed to that celestial felicity which God has prepared for his elect. Whoever desires to attain that must restrain the natural thirst for the enjoyments of life, and attend to the faithful discharge of the duties of his condition.

THE CATHOLIC BRIDE. 61

For you these duties are (in addition to those which religion prescribes for every person and class) to love your husband whom God has given you, to divide this love with no other being; to take care of your domestic affairs; not to disdain those household occupations which, as proper to your sex, are honorable to a lady of the highest rank; to rear up in the service of God the children you may be blessed with, and to inspire them with patriotic sentiments becoming true Christians and good citizens. To give edifying example to all your equals, of humility, meekness, charity, modesty, religion, chastity. And if you devote yourself to the various and important duties of your family, you will have little time to seek after the numberless pleasures of the world, which only tend to enervate the strongest mind, and impede the proper discharge of duty. Walk on, then, courageously towards your goal, and dally not among the roses that bedeck the way.

Do I mean by this, that while your path is, every where, surrounded by blooming flowers, you are forbidden ever to stoop and pluck some of them, as you hurry on? This, in sooth, would be extreme rigor. The pilgrim who "faints not" in his speed, nor checks his onward course, may, nevertheless, cull some flowers that fringe the way-side. This is not forbidn. For, among those flowers are some planted by God's own hands to cheer and sweeten the weary pilgrimage of life: but there are others planted by "the enemy;" and these are surrounded with venomous thorns, and their odor is not sweet. Wo to her who culls them! It is true, that those planted by God are not without their thorns, thorns which sprang up under the guilty touch of Eve, when she plucked the fatal apple. And, therefore, not only should you not linger among them, but you should walk, with great caution, amidst the thorns of so many, and stretch your hand to those only that are pure, and intact. To speak more plainly, avoid every enjoyment that might sully your fair soul: shun the continued dissipations of the midnight banquet, and the luxurious festival, little becoming the position of a Christian bride; avoid unseemly dress, and meretricious adornment; turn a deaf ear to the language of gallantry; and let the guardian of your person and your home be gentle modesty. As there is no good in the world that may not be changed into evil, moderation and temperance are indispensable, in all your recreations. There is danger every where. And even where it is not seen, yet is it to be feared. Even the chastest affections of the heart must be cherished with caution. This caution, however, is not too difficult to be observed: and when observed, it preserves the grace of God, gives light and strength; governs every affection, moderates every emotion of the heart, and guides every action of life. It keeps alive, in the breast, the flame of divine love, by which all other love, how pure or chaste soever, must be kept in perpetual subjection.

I fear I have trespassed beyond the limits of my duty. Yet I feel, most noble lady, that while you give your virgin heart to your illustrious husband, you will not reject my salutary counsels. I am aware that you do not stand in need of them: the admonitions and admirable example of your parents, the cultivation of your mind, your eminently Christian education, and the unsullied virtues of the family with which you are on the point of connecting yourself, render my suggestions unnecessary. Excuse them: they

THE CATHOLIC BRIDE. 65

are the expression of the thoughts of one, whose humble prayers will never cease to implore upon you, in your new and holy state, every temporal and eternal benediction. With a heart filled with pleasing hopes, and with sentiments of profound esteem and respect,

  Your humble
   And devoted servant,
    GIUSEPPE FRASSINETTI,
     Prior of St. Sabina.

GENOA, *August 4th,* 1845.

LETTER V.

FROM SILVIO PELLICO.

I AM permitted, by your truly excellent father, my dear young countess, to offer you my homages on the occasion of your marriage. And my pleasure in so doing is the greater, as I am but mingling my blessings with those which others have already invoked upon your youth, your virtues, and your joys. What we know of yourself, of your husband, and of both your families, combines to give us a consoling idea of those moral and Christian harmonies, which augur for the newly-married the greatest probability of future happiness.

But another, and still stronger ground of happy anticipation, is the finished education which you have received, as well under your parental roof, as under the care of the ladies of the Sacred Heart. With the principles which they have instilled into you, with the instruction you have acquired, with the habits of the purest affection and the tenderest piety, how can you prove otherwise than an excellent wife, and, should heaven bless your union with children, of an exemplary mother

The very gifts of a cheerful disposition, which God has blessed you with, derive a positive value when they are sanctified by the noble qualities of the mind. Cheerfulness and the sweet graces of gentle mirth contribute, in the young, who are the friends of God, to temper the wisdom of their conduct, and their contempt of vanity. These gifts are then a spectacle of edification, and an enchantment, by which others are persuaded to practise virtue, and love religion. I do not wish to flatter you, young countess; but the Lord has been bountiful in his gifts to you, and I trust that you will correspond to the divine favors you have received. No daughter has ever been blessed with a better mother: the worthiest daughters are they who imitate the virtues of their mothers.

I do not assert this merely as a sentiment founded upon reasoning, but with the lively conviction from the recollection of a case in point. Many years ago I found myself in relation with a pious family, in which was consummated a marriage fraught with pleasing hopes, but which, however, awoke some uneasiness in the parents' minds, on account of the extreme youth of the bride. I was present, one day, when a venerable priest, a relative of the family, ventured to express some affectionate misgivings arising from her inexperience, when she, with great candor, remarked, that she was not as inexperienced as he imagined. "And from whom, then," he asked, " have you learned to regulate your life?" " From my mother," was her memorable answer.

I was then too young to reflect; but still that simple and sublime reply did not fail to strike my mind, and very often since has it come back to my recollection. A bride, as yet almost in childhood, felt herself strong and courageous from the example of her mother's virtues! Difficulties and troubles were not wanting, in after life, to that excellent woman, and more, perhaps, than she could have foreseen; yet all her acquaintances admired the wisdom which she evinced from the beginning of her conjugal career, and the discretion, and fortitude, and amiable pru dence, with which she performed the duties of her state. She governed and obeyed, with the humility of a wife, but with great firmness, too, in the practice of good works. This was one of the few marriages of which I saw and admired the propitious results. There will always be, in the happiest, abundant occasions of sorrow: but, in this mortal condition we will surely find felicity to exist where the consolations of virtue are at hand.

When one advanced in age as I am, addresses a lady just on the eve of being led to the hymeneal altar, he cannot but yield to a kind of paternal instinct that warms the heart of age with sympathy for the young, and prompts him to suggest appropriate advice, although, perhaps, not necessary, and certainly not new. Although having no authority over you, permit me, gentle lady, to offer you one. I cannot forget that it would be useless to dwell upon others more essential, which, I have no doubt, you have already received, and still receive, from the dear and venerable minds of those who are so much better able to instruct you.

It seems to me that among the human virtues there is one too rarely recommended: and that is tranquil cheerfulness, continued serenity: that amiable, indulgent, and beneficent peace, which we love to contemplate as depicted in the countenances of the Angels, of Blessed Mary, and of the divine Redeemer himself. Oh sacred graces of virtue that is cheerful! But, perhaps, you smile, and answer: "this young heart that beats so merrily has no need of being excited to gladness: and, perhaps, greater gravity should be recommended to me."

Certainly, young countess, mirth, and joyous confidence, and smiles, are proper to your age: and a soul so pure and loving, feels a stronger tendency to gaiety and jubilee, than to grief and despondency. Certainly the nuptials on which you are entering are beaming with a thousand rays, and prognosticate a charming future. But alas! the most fortunate existence is composed of many elements. The relations and social ties of a wife become numerous and multiform, from the day she leaves her home to grace her husband's days, to assume the mother's cares, to preside over the family circle, to edify all, of every rank, under whose observation she may be placed. The quiet of her virgin days, of her peaceful retirement, of the gentle vigilance of her parents' and her teachers' solicitude are gone: those days are but a pleasing remembrance.

A child, it is true, is strengthened by her mother's example, we know: but will it always be an easy task to follow that, without apprehension? Oh! if virtue could enjoy uninterrupted content, where would be the merit of holy mirth? Is it to be supposed that the bride becomes a queen, and takes command in such a manner, that every thing must smile, and grow gay, before her joyous bidding. No, this is not, this should not be, the case. To the obligation of filial obedience, there is added another law of obedience, not less sacred, not less lasting, and, assuredly more serious, though sweetened by the affections. Illusory is that appearance of greater freedom that shines around the persons of the married. The condition of the wife is a condition of dependence, but of noble dependence. It is necessary that she who is placed in it should love it, and seek all her satisfaction in it.

Oh the humble peace of the years of childhood! the sweet obscurity of a virgin, who is not oppressed with brilliant, but yet thorny duties. The spontaneous ebullitions of those unsophisticated joys which every day brought forth, and which survived the season of infancy! ... But vain regret! Time will not retrocede: the period hastens on when the child becomes an adult, known to the world, exposed to its opinions, and subject to innumerable obligations. Behold life commences! Behold perpetual obedience! Behold the cross, to be carried by the most delicate of Eve's daughters. And, nevertheless, it is their duty to prove themselves heroines of patience, and love of tears, and contentment.

My dear countess, there are, in this pilgrimage, some paths less rough than others; and earnestly do I hope that yours will prove one most strewn with flowers, and most varied with pleasant scenes, and auspicious events. All this I augur for you, if you but carry out the beautiful monition of the Royal Psalmist: "Serve the Lord in joyfulness." The advice which I have given is but a commentary on his. Never, then, give way to lengthened complaints, or protracted sorrows. Adorn all your social and domestic duties with that happy disposition which we are wont to style good humor, and good will. This is one of the angelical traits which is natural to your character: you have not, therefore, to acquire it, but only to preserve the treasure you already possess. A soul habituated to benevolent gaiety, is a power. This heavenly serenity enlarges the horizon of the intellect and heart, subdues all obstacles, increases the motives of consolation, and wins over the minds of others to mildness, to thankfulness, and to virtue.

Blessed and lasting joy be with you, most gentle bride. Serve God, with calm content, amid all the cares of your new state of life, and spread around you, as you have hitherto done, meekness, and peace, the love of perfection, and the smiles of happiness.

 I have the honor to be,
   With great respect, &c.
      SILVIO PELLICO.
TURIN, *August 6th,* 1845.

LETTER VI.

FROM THE BISHOP OF ASTI.

SO FAIR a flower of your distinguished family, as you, young Julia, a flower which grew and was fostered, under a father's care in the garden of home, and, afterwards, expanded and blossomed under the cultivation of the Virgin Sisters of the Sacred Heart, cannot fail to diffuse the sweetest fragrance, and prove a consolation to your illustrious family, and an ornament to the bridal hall. And heaven will bestow those fruits, invoked upon you, by the benediction of that nuptial tie, which binds you to your excellent spouse. May you be enriched with its choicest blessings, and its fertile dews.

Meanwhile, permit me to share in the common exultation at your truly auspicious marriage: and I beg you to accept the following tribute, a familiar essay made up of some reflections on moral education; a subject which should claim the attention of every philanthropist, and of every Christian.

May your days be, ever, as fortunate and happy, as I can wish them to be, while I invoke upon you the benedictions of heaven.

† Filippo, *Bishop of Asti.*

MORAL REFLECTIONS.
BY THE SAME.

I am in the habit of contemplating, with astonishment, those prodigies of painting and sculpture which adorn our churches, our galleries, and the palaces of the great: and I cannot but reflect how persevering has been the industry of their authors, whose works, as it were, animated with being, are destined to be immortal. And I am led to say to myself: why is it that the rough canvass and the cold marble are wrought into the perfect resemblance of men, while parents often take but little, if any, pains to preserve in their children the original likeness and lineaments of men! Here, such a variety of coloring and shades, or such untiring patience in the use of the chisel, lest there should be the slightest want of symmetry, of expression, and, especially, of the character of the figures which start into life under the art of the painter or the sculptor: and, in parents, no care to form the traits and conduct of their children according to a truly Christian model, and, often so lamentable a neglect of it, that their offspring, deformed by the ugliness of every vice, hardly retain the image of Himself which God engraved on their foreheads; and grow up a curse to society, and a scandal to religion! How is that man, who, if I may thus speak, imparts education to inanimate and irrational nature, who compels the earth to supply his alimentary wants; the plants to lose, by cultivation, their original wildness; the elements—air, water, fire, gas, vapor—to minister to his ends; the deadliest poisons to assume the character of sanitary remedies;—how is it, that man who can tame the savage beasts, can yoke the ox, and bridle the steed, and chain the lion, and cage the tiger, and goad the elephant;—that man, not satisfied with ruling the earth, and extending his dominion upon the sea, but scans the very heavens, reaching the stars, and commanding the sun,—that man, in a word, who, by education, conquers and masters every thing, bestows so little thought upon the education of his children, the tender offspring of his own person? Ah! in vain, says the author of Ecclesiasticus, in vain do you put your hopes and your delight in your children, if they are not brought up in the fear of God. The fear of God is the source of all wisdom. But in the estimation of some, this is regarded as an obsolete truth, a maxim no longer in use, and by such education is neglected. That kind of education, I mean, which contemplates, especially, the government of the heart, and the formation of morals; and which, if not cherished, in families, as the root and nutriment of learning, will be inculcated, in vain, from the pulpit and the altar. This Christian education is very different from that external probity, which teaches men to appear, but not in reality to be, profoundly virtuous.; education, without which the most interesting qualities of the child—genius, beauty, and acquirements, will become the fatal instruments of refined destruction; education, in fine, which parents are bound to give, whose authority is the purest and most ancient image of the divine authority, and who are, accordingly, styled "visible gods" of their families, by the sacred Scriptures. A thousand times blessed are those children who are born in the bosom of a truly pious family! They will, one day, become parents, too, of children, who will be the consolation of their families, of the church, and of their country.

You, dear Julia, who have been favored with so rare a treasure, have only to call to mind how you have been educated by your excellent parents, in order to educate well the children whom heaven may design to bless you with. And as the example of the faults of others is a lesson in the school of virtue,—going, as you are, from the bosom of your family, which I venerate as the sanctuary of the Christian and social virtues, to the bridal hall, I request you to make, with me, as with others who are truly wise, some familiar reflections on the education of children. And like the dove that went from the ark, you will perch on the olive tree, view, with commiseration, the clod which you have left under your feet, and carry aloft with you, into your native air some of the branches of that tree of peace, which, at a later period, will impart solace and honor to the declining years of your beloved parents.

The universal Father of all mankind, God, deigned to make fathers his companions in the government of families: and Jesus Christ associated them, in some measure, with himself, in quality of Redeemer, because they are, together with himself, saviours of their own children. Because he confirms in heaven the commands given by them, entices children by the promise of the sweetest rewards, and terrifies them by the menaces of the severest punishments: he blends his benediction with that of the parents, and declares that the malediction of a mother will exterminate a family. Sacred and precious is the treasure which parents receive, as it were on deposite, in the children that are born to them: and they will be required to restore it to God, before they are rewarded or punished for the manner in which they have preserved it. If even a careful education is, sometimes not sufficient to guard the virtues of childhood against the vices of youth, what will be the case, if through the fault of parents, the burning passions take possession of a heart void of all religious convictions, and a stranger to the fear of God : or, if by an opposite extreme, equally to be deplored, they place their children, from their cradle, in the way of perdition, which will be pursued even to the tomb.

One word concerning the different classes of parents. There are some so very cruel, that it would seem they have given life to their children only to torment them: these are impetuous and austere, and will make no allowances for the weaknesses of their age, and make no concession to their reasonable desires. There are others, too easy and condescending, who love their children with a blind affection, and refuse them nothing. There are others so avaricious, that by their closeness and penurious rigor, they keep their children in a low and vulgar condition, where they form friendships fatal, at once, to their honor and their fortune. On the contrary, there are others who are voluptuaries, and bequeathe no other legacy to their children, than the pernicious example of their gratifications, and the torture of not being able to emulate them. There are others capricious and unjust, who, lavishing their favors upon one darling child, make the others victims of an unhappy aversion, which begets rancor, envy, and fraternal discord. There is an infinite variety of others, whom I should not style by the name of fathers, but tyrants of their families, who draw out, as if from the urn of fate, the destiny of their children, and bind them like slaves to that profession, to which neither nature nor heaven has called them: one to the bar, another to the camp, another to the marriage state, and another, from his very cradle, to the sanctuary or the cloister: and thus do they raise a sacrilegious hand to strike some Isaac, contrary to the will of heaven, and against his own consent. I trust there are few belonging to this inhuman class. And, yet, what do we see around us?—We see mothers, who, in order to rid themselves of the trouble of nursing their own offspring, consign them to the charge of mercenary hirelings, from whose breasts they suck with their milk, vulgar prejudices, and plebeian errors; and what is still worse, (if what is related of Alexander the Great be true; that he was a drunkard and died of the effects of wine, because he had been suckled by a woman who indulged too freely in its use,) to servants and uncouth domestics, who, too often, are destitute of probity, and calculated to spoil the finest disposition; who found their hopes on the caprices and disorders of the rising rulers of the house, whom they incite to evil in order to reap the fruits of their own malice; to the hands of stran gers, in fine, who are paid to keep the children at a distance from their parents, and who earn for them, in a certain manner, the right of forgetting them; erroneously persuading themselves that the burden will be light to a stranger which they themselves consider too heavy to be borne, or that sordid interest will secure to their offspring that good, which the most sacred affection withholds from them. And even though, in spite of so many difficulties in the education of children, the result should turn out fortunately, what object have parents in bestowing it upon them? To provide every thing for them except what relates to God. They seem to fear that piety would disgrace them in the world, to please which, they yield to all that it exacts, and do not hesitate to color its vices with attractive names. Dissipation they style urbanity, ambition magnanimity, immodesty levity, rashness courage, obstinacy constancy, prodigality goodness of heart, gallantry amiability. And, on the contrary, not satisfied with this deception, they vilify virtue, by calling temperance rusticity, modesty vulgarity, forgiveness cowardice, and respect for the clergy, devotion at church, and the frequentation of the sacraments, bigotry and simplicity. They rejoice, in their hearts, to see their children grow up independent, loquacious, disdainful of advice and correction, provided they can glitter in society. Unhappy parents! Too late do they reap the bitter fruits of such an education. Let them wait until their children can throw off the parental yoke, and begin to feel that they have no farther need of their solicitude, let them wait till they are laboring under the infirmities of age, and then let them declare whether the education which the world prescribes, is such as their hearts would desire. Ah! when in a family the mother becomes decrepit, and the father unable to govern his house, they will be objects of contempt to their children; they will be compelled to drink of the bitter chalice of sorrow; but the fault will be their own. To them it may be said, the ingratitude of your children is the effect of your own folly. You have armed them against yourselves, and, too late do you think of that religion which you neglected to teach them. It is but natural that parents, who were so reckless, should be punished with rebellious children: and to no purpose do the Hagars complain of the Ishmaels, or the Jacobs of the Dinas, or the Davids of the Absaloms, if to themselves the irreligion and rebellion of their children can be imputed. And, in vain, will they have taught the theory of virtue and religion, if their example has destroyed the effect of their instructions. It is easier for children to imitate their parents than to believe them. They inherit their passions, and as they succeed to their name, so do they likewise to their vices, as has been well remarked by Salvian: and the sacred oracles tell us that the father will live in the son, and the mother in the daughter. A merciful judgment, sometimes, cuts off in his bloom, some son, ere the malice of his father could corrupt his spotless mind; and, sometimes, the too cruel love of a mother, by her excessive indulgence, sacrifices her daughter, the hope and beauty of the family, a victim to untimely disease. And what does it avail that her miserable parents bathe her cold ashes with their useless tears? Let them rather mourn over their own guilt, or, at least, over that weakness which was the cause of her early death. They have blighted the lovely flower which was destined to flourish in the dew of heaven.

Their house, accordingly, becomes solitary: among their palaces and treasures they seek, in vain, for a child of their love, who may inherit them, a likeness in whom they may be represented. In their stead, they see, at hand, strangers as it were grasping at the spoils, and, in their withered ears will ring the voice of their ancestors reproaching them for having sealed their tomb for ever! Should heaven permit them to enjoy the object of their most cruel indulgence, what use will they make of it? To render them the victims of the blindest affection. In them they will recognise no vice,—they will find an excuse and a palliation for every defect. Alas, how deluded! Should a servant of the house dare to strike their darling child, they would, instantly, inflict on that menial the severest chastisement: and while vice tyrannizes over them and leads them to ruin; whilst he is the prey to passions that consume him, they remain tranquil, and leave him to defend himself in the midst of all the dangers of the world, and of corrupt society. Do they, perhaps, confide in the virtuous disposition of their children? Ah! gloomy caverns, deep solitudes, sackcloth and ashes, could not, always, be a protection to the hermits of the desert or the ministers of the sanctuary, of whom some have perished in the shadow of the cloister, and at the foot of the altar: and notwithstanding this, can we entertain a hope that young worldlings, badly educated and trained up, will not fall? that the frail reed will not be snapped, by the whirlwind, that often tears from its roots the cedar of Lebanon? In the world every thing leads to seduction, and furnishes aliment to the passions. Conversation betrays it, company fosters it, fashion authorises it, interest inflames it, the example of many of the great and noble sustains and adds lustre to it. The fine arts themselves are, frequently, made the means of the corruption of the heart. Painting, sometimes, displays its beauteous colorings to this end: to this, full often, poesy spreads out all the graces of the muse, music sends forth all the harmonies of song; and marble and bronze are shaped into voluptuous forms, which art immortalizes, and the philosophy of fashion defends, and praises.

What then? must parents keep their children always shut up at home, or immured in cloisters? By no means. But they should treat the world as they would an enemy, and put into their hands a shield of defence against the dangers that surround them. Let us imitate the sparrow, said a great Italian orator. Do you not observe that bird, that makes himself a citizen of our roofs? He, sometimes lights upon the ground—poor little thing—forced by necessity to seek his sustenance there. But as he knows that the ground is, for him, a treacherous place, where nets are spread, and traps are set, to catch him, he is ever timid, looks carefully around him, and with the grain in his beak, flies back into the air. Thus we, who are made for heaven, should be as pilgrims on this faithless earth, until we return to our celestial country: and thus, we should be the masters, instead of the slaves, of this wretched world. The young, especially, as pliable as wax to every impression, should be fortified against the corruptions and passions of the world, particularly those that are pleasing, and apparently innocent. For it has been remarked, by a celebrated writer, that there are moments when the young mind is so disposed, that it will seize upon any thing that has the appearance of pleasure; not unlike a flower which is hardly blown ere it abandons itself, on its tender stem, to the first zephyr that passes over it, and carries off its sweetest fragrance. Ah! those dangerous moments when the passions begin to be developed, should be guarded with timid caution. For it is then that they are exposed to cunning wiles, or open malice; and parents should not forget the lines of the poet:

> How easily a high-born soul may be
> A captive taken, when it stands alone,
> And in the threatening danger there is none
> To shield and save it from the enemy:

I am aware that the greatest vigilance of parents cannot rescue their children from the perils that beset them: but I, likewise, know that children who have received a proper education, do not begin to sin without trembling; and when their passions cool, their piety and reason warm up, anew, the sacred fire in their breasts, which has not been extinguished, but smothered for a time. Nor am I ignorant, that the best parents, sometimes, are not blessed in the conduct of their children: but, frequently, their prayers will ultimately effect what their precepts could not accomplish. The prayer of Monica—that unceasing and victorious prayer which won Augustine to the church—will stand a perpetual monument to such parents, of instruction and of consolation.

For the rest, if Quintilian, when he saw the youth of Rome becoming a prey to voluptuousness, foretold, that that boundless empire, the mistress of the world, would fall under the weight of her own vices; if inflamed with patriotic love, and magnanimous courage, he dared attribute their vices to the example of their parents, and to denounce the licentiousness of manners that prevailed, until Rome cried out for incorruptible judges, intrepid soldiers, worthy citizens, and the return of her primeval virtues and glory—if, I say, Quintilian acted thus, what can we, enlightened by the Gospel, anticipate for our country, or the church, when we behold the spectacle of corruption that has spread among our youth? Or what can we say of parents who style themselves Catholics —vicious parents of a more vicious offspring—but repeat the predictions of Horace to the Romans of his time.

Since, then, all the virtues of rightly educated children will be reputed as a crown and reward to their parents, so shall the vices of the former redound to the condemnation of the latter: for at their hands God shall require the blood of their children. And although they themselves might have been virtuous, their virtues will avail them nought, if they neglected to educate their children in the fear of God.

What would be sufficient to sanctify a Levite in the temple, a solitary or a virgin in the cloister, will not suffice for the salvation of a father or mother of a family. Because they owe to nature, to society, and to religion, the proper education of their children. And, although the laws of men be silent, children themselves who have been betrayed by their parents, will cry to heaven for vengeance. We had fathers, they will say, but rather were they our executioners. By their example, or by their connivance, they led us to the path of perdition. They gave us the life of the body only to deprive us of that of the soul. Cursed be the day on which they ushered us into the world! Cursed their love which has brought down upon us the hatred of our heavenly Father!

But these lamentations are little in accordance with your nuptial joys, respected Julia. My soul takes courage, and is comforted, at the sacred union which you have entered upon with your distinguished spouse, a true model of husbands, who are dear to mortals and loved by angels. If piously educated children be the glory of their fathers, as we are informed by the sacred oracles, your illustrious parents have, thus far, reaped the sweetest fruits of their care and affection: fruits which you yourself must, likewise, partake of: for, replete with pious hopes are the eulogies lavished by Solomon, in the name of God, upon a wise and "valiant" woman: she will secure the happiness of her home, she will be a blessing to her husband's heart, she will smooth the cares of the conjugal state, she will infuse sweetness into the bitterness of life's chalice, and she will surround and adorn her chamber "with young olives"—the lovely children with which heaven shall bless her love.

† FILIPPO, *Bishop of Asti.*

FROM THE REVEREND FILIPPO STORACE.

Illustrious Lady:

AMID the rejoicings and festivities of these auspicious days, in which all your friends participate, in consequence of your marriage with the excellent Count de Castelmagno, it would ill become me not to partake largely of the common joy and exultation, who am bound by so many endearing ties of benevolence, and of gratitude, to your distinguished family: to your loving parents, flowers of nobility and refinement, and rare and brilliant models of every civic and religious virtue. Leaving, however, to others, the pleasure of tendering their elegant congratulations on a union so happily concerted, and on the admirable qualities of your spouse, and, of course, on the splendid future, which, by God's kind favor, dawns upon your hopes; I prefer to mingle my rejoicings on another account,—that at your nuptials, as of yore, at those of Cana, I see, in spirit, our divine Redeemer presiding, in company with his blessed mother.

You readily understand my meaning. For, thoroughly, is your heart convinced of the necessity of a pure and holy intention, while standing at the foot of the bridal altar. While too many young ladies of your age enter upon the marriage state for the mere motive of enjoying a certain freedom from restriction, or from a romantic desire of making their appearance on the stage of the world, you, who have been taught better lessons, in the act of binding yourself with these indissoluble chains, will not fail to keep the eyes of your mind raised up to heaven. Faithful to the first inspirations which you imbibed with your mother's milk, the germs of holy thoughts and chaste affections which, cultivated afterwards under the shadow of the Sacred Heart of Jesus,* brought forth an abundance of pious fruits, you would not have taken any step, in this most important affair, without first consulting the will of God. This is acting wisely. For here below we are all pilgrims, hurrying on, at a rapid pace, to a blissful eternity. But wo to us, if, instead of leaving to God to point out the path in which we should walk, we presume to make the choice, of our own will and caprice. It is written that every tree that is not planted by the Almighty's hand, shall be cut down. There are

* Alluding to the convent of the Ladies of the Sacred Heart, where she was educated.

twelve gates, it is true, that lead into the heavenly Jerusalem, but it belongs to God to open one rather than another. He calls us all, by different ways, to his kingdom: some amid the splendors of a throne; others in the humility and obscurity of the cloister; others in the enjoyment of riches; others in the privations and sorrows of poverty; one with the spotless purity of virginity; and another, in fine, with the immaculate sanctity of the marriage state.

Each one, says the apostle, has his peculiar gift from God. And she alone can be confident of having made a proper use of that gift, who is guided in it, after fervent prayers and mature deliberation, by the wise suggestions of her parents.

Let us, then, bless God, may I say in the language of St. Jane Frances of Chantal, addressed on a similar occasion to her second daughter, *for your having been so fortunate; dispose your heart to love Him more, and be more grateful to Him than ever. Let your only ambition, in future, be to distinguish yourself by your modesty and wisdom in the state of life which you have embraced, and to profess, openly and solemnly, your practice of Christian devotion and piety.*

It should be the glory of a young lady to shed around her the sweet fragrance of virtue, the aroma of heaven, the balm of paradise. The more elevated her rank in society, the brighter should be the light, the more brilliant the splendor, of her actions. Let your light shine before men, says our Saviour, that they may see your good works; that is, as some of the fathers expound the text, that they may imitate them, and thus glorify your Father who is in heaven.

Wherefore St. Chrysostom has added: "I prefer to find distinguished for their many virtues those who inhabit large cities, than those who spend their lives in the desert. And why? Because from the example of the former much greater benefit is derived, as they do not light their candle to put it under a bushel. I would that every candle were placed on the candlestick, in order that it might spread abroad the rays of its light.

"Let it not be said: I am now married, I have my children to educate, my family to take care of, and how can I find time for the practice of the virtues? If all these concerns were no impediment in your way, nevertheless, if irresolute and tepid, you would not give yourself to acts of virtue; whereas, on the other hand, if you possess an upright and courageous soul, those domestic cares will be no hinderance to the cultivation of devotion. All that is required is the will of a strong and generous mind, and, then, neither youth nor age, nor poverty, nor wealth, nor multiplicity of occupations, nor any thing else will prevent you from applying yourself to the exercise of virtue."*

Devotion does not debase or humble the human character, as the enemies of religion pretend: in order the more effectually to attack and combat it, they represent it as the portion of abject and timid minds. They are in the habit of giving to words any meaning but their natural one, and, thus, wage a war, founded upon their false paralogism, upon the thing itself. When, therefore, they attack devotion, they admire it in their hearts as the basis of all virtues, but in order to impugn it with safety, they call it delusion, hypocrisy, imposture; they make a rule of the exception, and confound with virtue itself the abuse which is sometimes made of it; and because they may have detected that

* In Math. num. 43, 44.

abuse in some devotees, they fancy they have achieved a triumph over devotion itself.

But you well know what true devotion is. Nothing else, according to the definition of St. Francis of Sales, than a general inclination and power of our soul, to do what we know is pleasing to God. Now I ask: can there be any exercise, study, or disposition more noble, more sublime than this, or more congenial to a matron, a lady of refined spirit, cultivated manners, and lofty sentiments? St. Augustine observed with a *concetto* worthy of himself, that to serve God is to reign Seneca, the pagan, who was irradiated only by the light of nature, affirmed, that obedience to God is perfect liberty. A simple creature, a vile worm that crawls on the earth, man, who has nothing of himself, not even existence, is called to serve that glorious Being, whose glory, in the words of the Scripture, the heavens proclaim: that terrible Lord and almighty Sovereign of the universe, whose magnificence extends infinitely beyond the firmament, whose wisdom knows no limits, and whose goodness and mercy surpass all measure! And can we imagine any act more worthy of our intelligence, than to honor, serve, and love so great a Being, to whose worship and service the affections of our hearts so naturally tend.

Continue, then, with a frank and generous soul, illustrious lady, the path upon which you have entered: stir up, to this end, all the energies of your courageous heart, and glory, with the Apostle, in Christ, and in him crucified. And the more conspicuously that divine lover of your soul has signalised you, in society by the most brilliant qualities and gifts, the more pride should you take in always displaying the conduct of a true, Christian, the sincere disciple of Jesus, by the constant and assiduous practice of piety and devotion.

Devotion, the purest fountain of undefiled religion, inspires the wish and the resolution to give to God what belongs to God. The humble oblation of yourself to him when you awake in the morning, the daily attendance at the sacrifice of the mass (as far as practicable), the attentive reading of spiritual books, and, especially, an habitual regard to the presence of that infinite Majesty who sees all things, fervent aspirations and ejaculations to the heart of our Saviour, frequent reception of the holy Eucharist, and other acts of true and enlightened piety, for which you can always find leisure, in the midst of the numerous and necessary occupations of your family.

Devotion, the daughter of charity, makes you all to all, without ceasing to be wholly His, to whom you have consecrated your being. Man, writes St. Francis of Sales, may be, at the same time, entirely God's, entirely his father's, his mother's, his children's, his friends', in such a manner that, being all to each, he may likewise be all to all. Because the duty which makes him all to some, is not contrary to that which makes him all to all: provided that what is given to God in preference to every thing else cannot be taken from him by any other love. And no love can separate our hearts from God, except that which is contrary to him.*

Devotion, the school of perfection, accompanies and directs even the most ordinary and indifferent actions, referring all to the intention of pleasing and glorifying God, according to the counsel of the apostle: "Whether you eat or drink, do all things for the glory of God."

* Treatise of the Love of God, book x, ch. 8.

Devotion, the principle of order, assigns to every moment of time its proper measure, so that the fulfilling your duties to God will not interfere with those you owe your husband, your family, your parents, your friends, nor with the reasonable amusements of society. And, on the contrary, the fulfilling of the social duties will never prevent you from attending to those of religion and piety.

Devotion, the inspirer of sound prudence, gives such a character to every circumstance, to the richness of dress, reciprocity of visits, enjoyment of lawful amusements, and the very practice of devout exercises, that, observing, in all, a wise moderation, it must command the respect of the judicious and discreet. It prescribes, on all occasions, the rule which St. Louis, king of France, adopted with regard to his dress: that every person should dress according to his rank; so that the wise and good can never say: you go to extremes; nor the young: your fashion is too loose. But when the young will not be satisfied with what is proper, they should be governed by the maxims of the wise.*

Devotion, in fine, is the mother of holy modesty, the loveliest ornament of the sex. You, excellent lady, are so striking and brilliant an example of this virtue, that your presence alone is sufficient to check and condemn the dissolute. In you this virtue appears, in the manner of your dress, and in eschewing, in the decoration of your person, whatever might become a rock of scandal, to others. Even amid the darkness of paganism, Meleppa, the Pythagorean, wrote, in the following terms, to Chares: " a wise and virtuous woman should always have an eye to modesty in her dress, and not to magnifi-

* In his work entitled " Philothea."

cence. She looks for propriety, and the severest decency, and never admits those meretricious and superfluous ornaments which luxury has invented, and which nature condemns."

These are a few of the principal characters of Christian devotion: of which, in your new state of life, you should continue to make a public and candid profession, without the least dissimulation, or concealment.

'Perhaps there may be some under whose eyes my letter may fall, who will be inclined to smile, if not with derision, at least with pity, at my inculcating devotion and piety, on the festive occasion of your nuptials. But, I feel convinced, that the subject is peculiarly appropriate to the circumstances. If devotion be the gentle inclination of the heart to every legitimate affection, if it be the prompting of the will to discharge every honest duty,

THE CATHOLIC BRIDE. 115

why consider it ill-timed to inspire you, at this happy juncture, with holy love, and recommend the proper exercise of it on that solemn act of union, which kindles the chaste flame that is intended to consume two hearts in mystic holocaust? Far from me, indeed, be the austerity and rigor, that would interfere with the customary rejoicings and celebrations on such joyous occasions. Still, I cannot forget, in the midst of all these festivities, that there is nothing that adds so much to the spontaneous hilarity of the heart, and the lasting content of the newly married pair, as the practice of enlightened piety and true devotion

Is it not the first duty of a Christian bride to cherish the deepest sympathy, the tenderest affection for her husband. To devote herself, with all her solicitude, to the interests of her family? To bear, with patient fortitude, all the inconveniences inseparable from her state of life? To discharge, in fine, with dignified complacency, all the courtesies which society requires. Now devotion teaches and regulates all this. It may be said to resemble the manna of the desert, which suited all tastes, and satisfied all the various exigences of the people : in like manner does devotion adapt itself to all the decorums and requirements of social life. Thrice happy the bride, who, submitting her will to the law of God, consecrates herself, with a devout and generous soul, to the observance of it, in all its extension. Like the noble tree planted by the water side, she will bear, in the proper season, abundant fruits. The devout woman of the Gospel, is the valiant woman of the Proverbs. But where is the man who would not go to the utmost boundaries of the earth in quest of her whose price is beyond all value: she who possesses devotion, is blessed with that inestimable treasure.

In proof of this truth, we have the history and example of many illustrious matrons, renowned for sanctity, and of some who are honored on our altars. In vain do men of the world attempt to depreciate this most beautiful gem of paradise: in vain do they pretend that devotion weakens the energies of the mind, when we remember the magnanimous courage and wondrous wisdom of Elizabeth, queen of Hungary; in vain do they affirm that it deadens the natural sensibilities of the heart, and stifles its affections, when we appeal to the tender love and unprecedented heroism of Clotilda, queen of France. In vain do they insist that, at least, it detracts from the refinement, polish, and elegance of life, when we read of the captivating manners, and admirable graces of Margaret of Savoy. Devotion is not opposed to moderate and becoming amusements: of this, the rule of life proposed to himself by the holy Count Eleazar de Province, bears unquestionable evidence: *I do not intend that my castle should be made a cloister, and that its inmates should live like hermits. There is no cause why they should not be gay, provided they do not what their consciences would condemn, or what would expose them to offend God.* The saintly Mary of Savoy, has beautifully and justly remarked, that *sincere devotion will make us happy both in this world and in the other.* And before her day, the inspired apostle had written: " piety is useful for all things."

I have but one more word to add: and that is to recommend to you the counsel of our own venerable Father Giacinto de S. Maria: *cherish a tender love for the blessed mother of God, a great dread of hell, an ardent longing after the joys of paradise, and a firm hope of obtaining them.* Illustrious lady, the love of Mary is the foundation and life of all true devotion : it is the test by which the genuine may be distinguished from the spurious. You who have ever fostered this love in your heart will not fail to express it with your lips, to manifest it in your actions. And, offering to that most holy virgin a fervent prayer for your future happiness, both here and hereafter,

  I have the honor to be,
   Your humble servant,
     Filippo Storace.
Genoa, *August* 9*th*, 1845.

FROM THE REVEREND G. AUDISIO.

Illustrious Julia:

YOU WERE, yesterday, a young maiden; you are, to-day, a young bride. Poetry has conducted you to the altar under a shower of garlands, and has evoked, on the occasion, symbols, images, and divinities, the creations of ingenious and brilliant fancy; but your intellect, your heart, your education, so eminently moral and religious, will not repose on the dreams of a day or an age. Nor would your taste, which delights to see wisdom united with beauty, be satisfied with a festive epithalium, beauteous only in its composition, were I to

offer such, amid the joyous circumstances of your nuptial union. This would not answer the expectations of your parents, who, with a true nobility of soul, and from their studies and pursuits, place more value on great and excellent actions, than on pompous and elegant words. Wherefore, I have determined to write you this letter, which I consecrate to your parents, in whom you honor, with so much reason, the earthly likeness of the heavenly divinity: and to yourself, whose piety, wisdom, character, manners, and person, render so distinguished and amiable a descendant of an ancient and glorious ancestry; and, in fine, to the husband whom God has chosen for you, whose virtues prove him worthy to become, in future, the cherished object of your love, and the sacred portion of your soul. I am aware that I can add little to the instructions you have already received from your enlightened mother, and less to the efficacy and sweetness of her language. It will be my purpose, therefore, merely to place before you anew the lessons which you have heard and learned from her lips, and which may be of use to others, whom Providence may unite in the same sacred and solemn bonds of marriage.

Tell me, then, by what ways your prudent mother, guided by the superior wisdom of her illustrious consort, disposed your virginal heart to make the solemn vow which you have taken at the altar? Aware that a young damsel, possessed of a light heart and a warm imagination, would not fix her affections on any one if they were divided and scattered among many, as well by her own care as by that of others, she watched over your soul, as a treasure confided to her by the Almighty. She permitted you to see enough of the world without being contaminated by its spirit: and so great was the fruit of her vigilance, that you can now offer to a husband the best gift of a virgin,—the plenitude of a pure and immaculate heart. An intelligent and careful observer of the divine will, she smoothed and illumined the path that was to lead to the choice of a partner for life: and, after the divine will manifested itself, she imparted to you those instructions on the marriage of a Christian, which she, herself, on a similar occasion, had derived from her respected mother. An hereditary wisdom, which you will transmit to future generations, and which will be, in the language of the wise man, like " grace added to thy head, and a chain of gold to thy neck."* Let us, then, collect those confidential admonitions; let us endeavor to awaken again that celestial harmony which your

* Prov. ch. i.

mother's voice poured into your reverent and sensitive heart.

"My daughter," did she say, "you were the first tender scion with which the Lord gladdened, in his verdant years, the affectionate heart of your father: and it increased and blossomed, pure as the lily, and lovely as the rose of morning. To you belonged the first fruit of our love, and you enjoyed it. You know how your father forgot in you, his anxieties of public life, how he caressed you as his darling, how you smiled upon him in your affection: and as your years increased, how he advised and directed you. Like a minister of Providence, an angel appointed to watch over your innocence, he protected and guided your earliest steps in the dangerous paths of life. I speak not of myself, I am your mother. It has now pleased God to put an end to our mission, but not to our love. He destines you, a new Sarah for a new Isaac; and we consign you, with our fervent vows, to his noble arms."

At these accents, so maternal, so holy, your heart dissolved, and your faltering voice, and streaming eyes bore testimony to your grief, your gratitude, your love. And your mother, pressing you more tenderly to her bosom, continued

"Have courage, my daughter, the delight and solace of my heart. Let us look up to heaven. Divided in body, in God we will continue united in mind and affection. The body is here below; life is a pilgrimage. But Him does the immortal soul contemplate; and that immortal essence sees in him, and, through him, holds converse with, spirits it holds dear. Praying and meditating, you will see your parents, and we will find our daughter. Our souls will commune together and be happy. This is the faith of

Christians, this is the consoling piety of relatives."

Other young ladies who give themselves up to thoughtless levity, but little understanding the greatness, the wonders, the beauty of that spirit which they leave uncultivated, will not taste the nectar of these sentiments. But you who have refined the arts and graces of life by the study of religion and the spirit of prayer, that precious gift of God, you reposed in them as in rays of light, and in the tranquillity of heavenly peace. Of which peace your loving instructress availing herself, resumed the tenor of her gentle instructions:

"My dearest daughter, by being united to God, nothing will prevent you from fulfilling his holy will; and his will is that heaven should be peopled with saints who will praise His name for ever. For this purpose, he moves and guides the globe of the earth. The souls of these saints he created to display their nobility, and excellence, and to preserve over them his universal and paternal dominion. But, for the minister of bodies he has deigned to associate with himself his own creatures: and thus to present, on earth, a visible image of that invisible paternity with which he rules from on high. To serve God is wisdom and sanctity. Virginity has been dear to you, and you cherished it as the loveliest flower of life, and you venerated it in those followers of the Lamb, who, having vowed it to God, exercise in the cloister, as it were, a minor priesthood, which confers on us the blessings of heaven; and those spirits, clad in the habiliments of the flesh, perform the duties of the angels of paradise. But since God has assigned another path to you, do not recede. Everywhere will you find God, and where God is, there must life and happiness be found."

On hearing such language, what were your sentiments? Whither did your imagination carry you? Ah! your thoughts and affections were borne to those blessed retreats where the followers of the Lamb mingle their divine canticle with the chorus of the saints, a canticle which will cease on earth only to be resumed in heaven. Your mind yearned towards that sacred convent which has been for you, as it were, a second mother, and where you have acquired that nice estimation of human things, which is far more easily lost than learned, amid the pomps of the world. Your example will prove whether the devotion of the cloister is the fostering of a sullen and inactive mysticism, or rather the admirable culture of the mind and the affections, the development and strengthening of the soul, by which you may withstand the painful sacrifices which virtue imposes on your sex, especially in the great lottery of life. From you the world will know, that the active solitude of the monastery is a better teacher of wisdom and virtue, Christian and social, than the pageantry of the theatre, or the dissipation of the ball-room. On this account did you love it; on this account did you ever cherish towards it a sweet and grateful recollection. But, let us follow the star that guides you on:

"From St. Jerome, who wrote, from his beloved Bethlehem, such heautiful strains, to the Paulas, the Fabias, the Eustachiums, the Demetrias, and other Roman virgins and matrons, I learned to make you love and admire God's precious book—the sacred Scriptures. When a child, how often have I held you on my knee, whilst I read its pages, explained its meaning, and impressed its facts and images upon your tender mind! In them you saw with what a manifestation of majestic dignity the Almighty created man, how he breathed his own breath into his nostrils; how he bade him stand erect, and look upwards to his native heaven, to whose immortal spheres the immortal soul aspires. But his goodness did not stop here. From the part of the body nearest the heart, he took a rib from man, and formed the woman. Poets and prosers have said excellent and derogatory things of us : yet, we remain as God has made us; that is, the work of his hands, and an integral part of man and humanity. Woman should not confide, too much, in poets, the eulogists and vituperators of our sex. One of them, alluding to the creation, has not hesitated to sing:

On sent qu'a ce chef-d'œuvre Il doit s'etre arrete.*
Pour son dernier ouvrage il crea la beaute :

God's last and loveliest work lo! beauty rose:
This chef-d'œuvre formed, twas meet he should repose

* *Le merite des femmes*, par Legouve.

It is true that woman was the last work of his creative hands. But think not, my daughter, that our mission here below is merely to glitter among men, arrayed in the smiles of vain and fragile beauty, or adorned with the hues and graces of elegant accomplishments. In such a case, what judgment would men form of us, in what estimation would they hold us; what would we ourselves do, worthy of the mind and heart which God has bestowed upon us? Would not men pass us by, as we pass by a useless flower, which we do not stoop to pluck? Did not the shameful traffic which the Roman women made of their beauty justly excite against them the sharp satire of Juvenal? And did not the female levity and folly of more recent days afford a theme for Boileau's muse, which we cannot read without shame?"

Do not be surprised, young countess,

if the meek spirit of your mother uttered
these words with a bosom heaving with
emotion, and an eye flashing with enthusiasm. Her object was to screen your
pure mind from the vicious and passion-
ate influence of the world. And to direct
it to the fulfilment of its real mission,
which is the basis and completion of its
glory, she continued thus:

"There is another beauteous trait which
we possess; one, too, that cannot be under-
valued or destroyed: and that is the deep
sentiment of love for our husbands and our
offspring, which nature has identified with
our being. God has said: it is not good
for man to be alone; let us make him a
help like unto himself. And the Lord
God built the rib which he took from
Adam into a woman, and brought her to
Adam, and Adam said: This now is the
bone of my bones, and the flesh of my
flesh: she shall be called woman because

she was taken out of man. Wherefore a man shall leave father and mother, and shall cleave to his wife, and they shall be two in one flesh.* Let us leave to poetry to imagine the beauty of innocent Eve. To us, her daughters, after so many centuries of sin and evil, it is of little avail to speak of it. Let us rather glory in the mission which is assigned us,—to constitute the noblest part of man, to aid and comfort him by a chaste and tender love, and to become the mothers of generations unborn. For this, did the hand of the Almighty create and bless us: this benediction consecrated marriage among the Patriarchs, which is raised to a much higher dignity among Christians. My daughter, I have one important truth to communicate to you: listen with all your attention.

"The eternal Word espoused to himself

* Genes. chap. ii.

human nature, and redeemed it. Then he instituted and espoused the church, on which he lavished the plenitude of his love. The apostle who unfolds, with inspired eloquence, the sublime philosophy of Christianity, has made a parallel so glorious to Christian marriage that, had it emanated from any other source, it would appear the language not so much of reality as of enthusiasm. He exalts and ennobles the marriage of Christians, by comparing it to the union of Christ with his church. Having condemned the works of the flesh which obscure the light of the intellect, and lead to infidelity, he exclaims: this is a great sacrament; but I speak in Christ and the church.* Such is the beautiful image which continually presented itself to the profound mind of St. Paul. He compared the two alliances, the old to the bondwoman, Agar, who

* Ephes. chap. v

brought forth children, but not free; the new, to the mystic Jerusalem, which is free, and the mother of the free. He styles the converts to the Gospel her children; for in Christ Jesus, by the Gospel, I have begotten you.* In like manner, in the estimation of all the Apostles, redemption is a divine generation, effected by grace and love. For, of his own will hath he begotton us, by the word of truth, writes St. James, that we might be some beginning of his creature.† And the prince of the apostles admonishes us, to desire the rational milk without guile, as new born babes.‡ Jesus Christ has, also, been pleased, with the parable of the nuptial feast, to shadow forth his loving invitations to our souls to be united with himself.§ Finally, not content with representing, under the symbol of marriage,

* 1 Cor. chap. iv.   † James, Ep. chap. i.
‡ 1 Ep. Pet. chap. ii.   § Math. chap. xxii.

the ineffable union of Christ with our souls, by virtue of his grace and his sacraments, the apostle of love has figured under it the glorious union to be consummated in heaven. Hear his magnificent language: And a voice came out from the throne, saying: give praise to our God, all ye his servants, and you that fear him, little and great. And I heard, as it were, the voice of a great multitude, and as the voice of many waters, and as the voice of great thunders, saying: Alleluia, for the Lord our God, the Almighty, hath reigned. Let us be glad and rejoice, and give glory to him: for the marriage of the Lamb is come, and his wife hath prepared herself. And it is granted to her, that she should clothe herself with fine linen, glittering and white, for the fine linen is the justification of the saints. And he said to me: blessed are they that are called to the marriage supper of the Lamb.*

"What is the meaning, my daughter, of such splendid rejoicings in the ever blessed mansions of paradise? Not on account of the commencement of his reign, but of the crowning of the church, the spouse of the Lamb,—and of the universal triumph of her children. Thus, as members of that church, are we all, married and single, espoused to Christ, in the bonds of faith and charity, and preparing to join in the nuptial alleluias which resound through the kingdom of heaven. And, that nothing may be wanting to perfect this sublime picture of Christian matrimony, I might depict, in purest colors, the immaculate virgin of Nazareth, crowned with lilies, and yet espoused to Joseph. I might display to you the value and sanctity of maternity, by the

* Apoc. chap. xix.

example of that divine infant, who knowing no father but in heaven, still did not refuse to reverence, in a woman on earth, the name and reality of his mother."

It is not difficult to divine the sublime thoughts which such considerations awoke in your mind. How beautiful, how holy is religion! you mused. Innocence crowned the nuptials of the first woman, amid the delights of Eden, and under those heavens that were still radiant with virginal light. The priest was the Eternal himself; and the altar two hearts as yet undefiled by the stain of sin. But grace, and the sacrament of the Gospel, raises to heaven itself the Christian nuptials, of which not only is God the priest, but the everlasting spouse: and *I will espouse thee to me for ever.** You, moreover, said: what purity of mind and body should I not carry with me to

* See chap. ii.

the nuptial altar! And your mother resumed:

"The church, the faithful guardian and interpreter of the divine mysteries, exhibits to our souls the dignity of the sacrament which she surrounds with the pomp of her ceremonies, and consecrates with the solemnities of her sacrifice. I always cherished a sentiment of gratitude towards an excellent priest, who presented me, in early life, a translation of the nuptial mass, as a preparation for marriage, which will be useful in disposing you to the same hallowed end.

"Often have I made you understand how the church, while she governs the heart, excites and elevates, likewise, the imagination. Her rites, her prayers, her hymns, show forth the poetry, and perpetuate the reminiscences, of the patriarchal times. The nuptial mass displays both, in a wonderful manner. It begins by repeating the words of the blessing which Rachel pronounced at the holy nuptials of Tobias with Sarah. The God of Israel join you together, and be with you. He who had pity on the two only begotten; and grant now, O Lord, that they may bless thee fully. And it adds, with the Psalmist: blessed are they who fear the Lord, and walk in his ways. Then the prayer is said: Hear us, omnipotent and most merciful God, that thy benediction may perfectly accomplish what is here administered by us. The fervor of your heart, my daughter, will accompany at the altar these fervent vows offered for you by the priest. You will invoke the protection of the angel who was the guide and companion of Tobias, and your confidence will be placed in him who had pity on his *only begotten:* a tender expression which nature cannot but treasure among its dearest reminiscences.

" All the ceremonies of the church are

moral, and eminently moral is the epistle of this mass, in which St. Paul delineates, with peculiar energy, the sublimely religious character of matrimony, the bond of which is love: Let women, he writes, be subject to their husbands as to the Lord—because the husband is the head of the wife; as Christ is the head of the church. He is the Saviour of his body. Therefore, as the church is subject to Christ; so also let the wives be to their husbands in all things. Husbands, love your wives, as Christ also loved the church, and delivered himself up for it, that he might sanctify it, cleansing it by the laver of water in the word of life; that he might present it to himself a glorious church, not having spot or wrinkle, nor any such thing: but that it should be holy and without blemish. So also ought men to love their wives as their own bodies. He that loveth his wife, loveth himself. For no man ever hated his own flesh: but nourisheth and cherisheth it, as also Christ doth the church: for we are members of his body, of his flesh, and of his bones. For this cause shall a man leave his father and mother; and shall adhere to his wife; and they shall be two in one flesh. This is a great sacrament: but I speak in Christ and in the church. Nevertheless, let every one of you in particular love his wife as himself: and let the wife reverence her husband.

"If with these precepts, so conformable to faith and nature, we compare, my daughter, the scandalous licentiousness which characterised the marriages of ancient Greece and Rome, we will clearly perceive the difference between the spirituality of Christian society, and the carnality of Pagan. From the latter, sprang forth dissoluteness which confounded the succession of families, and daily divorces, which extinguished the love of the parents, and that of the children. In the former, everything combines to effect a perfect unity: for we never can be happy if we divide our affections: and, like God, after whose image we are made, we concentrate in one object the past, the present, and the future. Hence our Maker, who well knew the wants of human nature, united, from the beginning, one man and one woman only: and this indissoluble unity the Apostle has figured under the sacred and perpetual union of Christ with his church. Hence, our gracious Redeemer, has laid down as an inviolable principle, that, *whom God hath united let no man put asunder.**

"And would you believe, beloved Julia, that the church holds these nuptials in such high estimation, that she directs the

* Matt. chap. xix.

priests to interrupt, so to speak, the awful sacrifice, in order to shower over the couple, prostrate at the foot of the altar, the benedictions of heaven. After the *pater noster*, the minister of religion offers this beautiful prayer: O God, who by thy power, didst bring forth all things out of nothing, and regulate the elements of the universe, who didst give unto man, made after thine own likeness, an inseparable help-mate in woman, taken from the flesh of man to show that what thou hast joined together should never be separated; O God, who didst consecrate matrimony by an excellent mystery, that of the sacrament of Christ with the church; O God, by whom the woman was made the spouse of the man, and this first and necessary state was sanctified by that blessing which hath not been destroyed either by the punishment of original sin, or by the waters of the deluge; thou, O God, deign to look down piteously upon thy handmaid, who, in the act of binding herself in the chains of matrimony, invokes the solace of thy grace. Bind her in the sweet yoke of charity and peace: may she be faithful and chaste in Christ Jesus, and imitate the example of holy wives. May she be amiable to her husband, like Rachel; prudent, like Rebecca; long-lived and faithful, like Sarah; and over her may the first author of prevarication have no power; may she persevere in the faith, and in the observance of the commandments. Bound to one husband, may she know no unlawful pleasures. Strengthen her infirmity with the rigor of duty: may she be grave on account of her modesty, venerable on account of her purity; sound in Christian doctrine, fruitful in her offspring, well-proved and irreprehensible, and bring them, at length, to the kingdom of the blessed, and the abode of the elect.

May they see their children's children to the third and fourth generation, and attain to a hoary age."

This prayer fell upon your soul, like the melodious tones of heaven. You promised to repeat it, with all the fervor of your heart, together with the priest, at the altar, in order that its divine auguries may be accomplished in you: and, embracing you with all the sympathies of her tender soul, your mother continued:

"My daughter, prayer is that mystic ladder by which our souls commune with God. To us women, he has given sensitive hearts, in order that we may the more ardently pray for parents, husbands, and children. As for yourself, this is the hour when your prayers should be most fervent and earnest. God has given this instruction to the married, in the person of Tobias, whose first words to Sarah were these: Sarah, arise and let us pray to

God to-day . . . . for we are the children of the saints, and we must not be joined together like heathens that know not God. So they both arose and prayed, and prayed earnestly. . . . And Tobias said: Lord, God of our fathers, may the heavens, and the earth, and the sea, and the fountains, and the rivers, and all thy creatures that are in them, bless thee. Thou madest Adam of the slime of the earth, and gavest him Eve as a helper. And now, O Lord, thou knowest that not for fleshy lust do I take my sister to wife, but only for the love of posterity, in which thy name may be blessed for ever and ever."

And Sarah, continuing her husband's prayer, said: have mercy on us, O Lord, have mercy on us, and let us grow old both together in health.* Their prayer was heard in heaven.

Prayer, the sacrament, and the sacrifice,

* Tobias, chap. viii.

warn you, my daughter, of the vast importance of the step you have taken for life. To honor your father and mother-in-law, to love your husband, to take care of the family, to govern the house, and to behave irreprehensibly, these are the admonitions with which Raguel and Anna gave away their daughter Sarah, and with them I give you, my beloved Julia. I pray that neither your youth, nor the example and vanities of the world will stain the spotless wreath of daughter, wife, or mother. Be obedient and respectful to your father and mother-in-law, show them every homage of reverence, by anticipating their wishes, respecting their counsels, sacrificing your pleasures and convenience to gratify them, and soothing and cheering, with peace and serenity, their declining days. Towards your husband act like the valiant woman so highly praised by the Holy Ghost: *In her the* *heart of her husband trusteth.*[*] Which sentence has been thus paraphrased by a poet.

Elle fixe chez lui la douce confiance
La tendresse et la paix, vrais biens de l'existence ;
Tempere ses chagrins, ajoute a ses plaisirs,
Soulage ses travaux, et remplit ses loisirs.

In him reposes the confiding wife,
With tenderness and peace—blest sweets of life:
Adds to his pleasures, tempers all his cares,
Soothes him in labor, and in leisure cheers.

As you are united in one sacrament, so should you be, likewise, in one mind, one will, one hope. Nothing should be concealed from each other; there should be a fellowship of sympathy and mutual aid; of consolations and joys, of sorrows and pains; for each other you should live with edification, and die with fidelity. The root and head of your family, your virtues or your vices will become the virtues or vices of your house, nay, also of your descendants. You will love your

[*] Prov. chap. xxxi.

children, who will be respectable in society, and pleasing to God and men in proportion to the care which you will have bestowed upon their education. On the wife, moreover, devolves the secondary management of the family, and the attention to domestic duties, which were not disdained by the Greek or Roman matrons, or the holy women of ancient times. Customs and manners vary more or less, but in spite of the increase of luxury and ease, the duties of the household should be assiduously attended to. And the language of the Holy Ghost is both morally and physically true: viz, that the wise woman buildeth her house, but the foolish will pull down with her hands that also which is built.*

Remember the wants of the poor, and relieve the miseries of the sick and abandoned. Let these suffering children of

* Prov. chap. xiv.

Christ form your second family; minister to their necessities, and be thankful to God for having given you the means by which you can contribute to aid and comfort them. And never forget the tender promise of Jesus Christ: amen I say unto you, whatsoever you have done to these little ones, you have done to me.*

Great virtue does not disdain small things, nor refuse to extend its influence to *little ones*. The first to reap the fruit of it will be your maids and servants. Affable, without familiarity, you will love them for God's sake, and provide for their corporal and spiritual wants, convinced that of them you will have to render a strict account on the last day. Let them never witness in you caprice, frivolity, or passion. Let your orders be precise, and give none except what they can and should obey. Admonish them mildly,

* Matt. chap. xxv.

and recompense them generously. Be tranquil in the midst of your most pressing occupations, and do everything in the proper time and place. Let religion and piety have their hours, and your acts of devotion be well-timed and judicious. Give to the duties of your family your first cares—in them God is always to be found. Make a constant study of yourself; mistrust flattery as no better than poison, and the person who admonishes you kindly esteem and be grateful to, as a sincere friend. Keep a secret with fidelity, and listen not to calumny and detraction. Let no artificial graces spoil the simplicity of your natural manners: elegance and dignity are inseparable from simplicity. Do not waste your time in reading romances. They vitiate the imagination, render the mind frivolous and light. Love history, which awards with rigid impartiality, the laurel to virtue, and condemns vice, no matter how glittering. But let the crown of every virtue be faith and Christian piety. Do not, however, dispute with those who are not under their holy influence, but evince, in their regard, your compassionate sorrow, and vindicate both with the arm of charity. Frequently peruse the writings of St. Francis of Sales, of St. Theresa, and study Fenelon's exquisite treatise on the education of young ladies.

Julia, one word more. You who are now just entering upon the path of life on which I am far advanced, profit by a mother's holy experience. Youth, parents, friends, every thing, are smiling upon you, like the beauteous morning of spring: but, be prepared for the autumn, nay, be prepared for the spring. Amid the flowers, and smiles of life, there will not be wanting thorns and tears, in this vale of grief. Your sex was the first to prevaricate, do not repine if it should be the first to suffer. Yet God has placed in your weak body a soul strong in endurance, an energy powerful to relieve the sorrows of another. The crown and joy of her husband in days of prosperity, an Iris of peace in the clouds that brood over families, the wife, with her affection and gentle sympathies, is his support, and the star of his faltering spirit amid the darkness and chances of life. She encourages his sinking heart. Woman drank the last dregs of sorrow in the chalice of her afflicted Son! Woman sustained and comforted him in his agonies; woman is the hope and beacon of the wave-tossed and desponding mariner on life's perilous sea. Around her is a halo of peace, serenity, and solace, as a mother and a wife, which sheds its benign light into the bosom of families. I have, thus far, spoken to you as a mother: will you not always be my darling daughter, Julia?"

It does not become me to penetrate farther into those retreats, or interrupt the sacred effusions of maternal and filial piety. Generous tears are ornaments to strong and generous souls: and woman is generous and strong. In her triple quality of daughter, spouse, and mother, she possesses a manliness of spirit, which is not her's, because it emanates from heaven. I might cite the noble example of Veturia who saved Rome from the vengeance of her son, whilst consuls, and tribunes, and the gods themselves, trembled in the capitol. I might cite that of Eponina, a prodigy of conjugal affection, who, during the space of nine years, in the bowels of the earth, amid ruins and ashes, clung to her beloved Sabinus, comforted, and consoled him, happy and faithful, in her subterranean exile, and more worthy of triumph, than of the cruel sword of Vespasian. I might refer to that of the shepherdess of Arc, who, for seventeen years, headed a valiant army, and unfurled the banner of France over a conquered foe, a martyr to her country, her religion, and her king. To the Judiths and the Esthers, who armed by prayer and fasting, displayed the graces of their sex, and the valor of heroes. The mother of the Macchabees, Symphorosa, Felicitas, and queen Blanche, who declared that she would rather see her son Louis fall dead at her feet than that he should commit a mortal sin: what language, what instruction, do not such women address to our hearts! And, in more recent days,—days of terror and woe, when fidelity to the sovereign and to religion was punishable with death, were there not women, daughters, wives, who, like the afflicted Mary, stood under the gibbet

on which the victims died. And when
the magnanimous Lefort having freed her
husband under the guise of a female, and
assumed his place in prison, was menaced
by the executioners in these words: *Malheureuse, qu'avois vous fait!* wretched woman, what have you done? She replied:
Mon devoir: fais le tien. My duty; do
yours! What encomium, or what benediction can I bestow on those virgin-disciples of Christ, who trampling upon their
worldly hopes and youth, for their salvation and that of others, buried themselves in solitude, and, as it were, in the
tomb: or on others, who rush into prisons, hospitals, and to the field of battle,
to minister to the distressed, and smooth
their dying pillow. And these, not from
the low, but the highest ranks of life,
even from magnificent thrones, like Mary
from the throne of heaven, imparting
blessings and solace to the desolate and

needy. In their hearts the oppressed find an asylum, the weak, strength. They catch the shriek of misery, and bear it to their husbands! And thousands might have reason to exclaim of each one:

Elle le fait cherir par ses bienfait nombreux:
Et le monarque est grand quand le peuple est heureux.

Through her benign persuasion gently moved,
He scatters blessings round, and is beloved:
A happy people make a monarch great. . . .

The wife has a dominion over the religious feelings and the heart of her husband. The first training of existence is in her hands. The sterner sex derives, from the maternal breast, those sparks of virtue and religion which will never be extinguished: and young maidens drink in that lively faith, that efficacious piety, which goes down from generation to generation. In the most skeptical age, woman will believe, because she stands in need of hope and charity for herself and others. Man may have charity on his lips, but it loses its power, amid the material avocations of society. Woman carries it in her heart and in her affections. Woman is the guardian angel of the people, under every circumstance: to the aged by her care, to wives and virgins by her advice, to orphans by her tender charity, to the poor, the wretched, the forsaken, in a thousand offices of sympathy and solace. She extends aid to all: procures work for some, education for others, gives alms and clothes to many, and compassion and sacred pity to all. The voice of woman is the sweetest melody to the ear of the miserable; for it is the voice of one who is tender, patient, prodigal of herself, from motives of pure and undefiled religion, concealing in God's just bosom the secret of her reward. Woman does not excite the envy which man can hardly escape. She continues, on earth,

THE CATHOLIC BRIDE.

the even career of her apostleship of faith and charity: and when the incredulity of man hurls down the fabric of society, woman flies to religion, and, with her heavenly aid, rears it up again in triumph, from its ruins.

Young and illustrious bride! behold your mission, behold the career to which God destines you; behold the preparation, the scope, and the manner, with which you should enter upon it! Let your models and guides be those two illustrious subalpine ladies, the Lodovichas and Clotildas; and the admirable and saintly queen of Hungary, of whose life and virtues your mother has given us so excellent a compend; and the translator of the Triumphs of Religion by Lancelot, and the thoughts of the venerable missionary of Beauprè: I mean your admirable mother.

From the Royal Basilick of Soperga,
Aug. 11, 1845.   GUGLIELMO AUDISIO.

LETTER IX.

FROM PROFESSOR CARLO FERRERI.

To the Countess Solaro della Margarita.

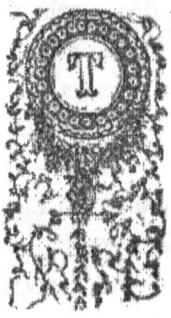THE congratulations which you receive, dear madam, from the priests and ministers of the sanctuary, on the occasion of the nuptials of your beloved Julia, are no small tribute to the excellent education, and edifying example, with which you have trained her up to virtue and to piety. And you may now, with reason, anticipate the most fortunate results to your country and the church. Silence, in the midst of the festive rejoicings of so many illustrious citizens, would ill comport with the spirit

of the Gospel, which is opposed to despondency and melancholy, and favorable to pure and holy joy, which in the good, is but the symbol of eternal bliss. Being myself, therefore, among the number of those who, through reverence and gratitude, are delighted with any happy occurrence, in your family, I cannot and should not be silent, whilst the accomplished Count Eduardo de Castelmagno leads to the altar, and selects as his companion for life, that gentle maiden whom, in the bloom of her years, you have made a rare example of every lovely virtue. Would that I could present you something new and worthy of this joyous occasion: but anxious as I am to do so, I feel that I can hardly give expression to the ardent desires of my heart. And yet, while thinking over in my mind what subject might be most appropriate and instructive, I remember a passage in the Life of Queen

Elizabeth, by the Duke de Montalembert, which you, madam, have so elegantly translated into Italian. Speaking of the influence which Catholicity spread over the world in the thirteenth century, that sublime and exquisite thinker remarks: that the *loftiest and most beautiful of all poetry is the liturgy of the church.* Reflecting on this noble sentiment, the idea in what manner I should present my homages to your pious daughter immediately occurred to me. I consulted the liturgy: and in the holy rite of matrimony, and in the unbloody sacrifice of the mass which is celebrated on the occasion, I seem to have found, as it were in the garden of the Lord a flower which will not be unacceptable to the friends of the Most High. I beg you, madam, to accept it: for, surrounded as you are by your favored and happy family, in the midst of so many Christian virtues, you will be able to testify, by your own example, whether it is in vain that matrimony is consecrated at the altar. Deign to read over that, which betokens such smiling and blessed hopes of the future, and present it to the young countess, as a pledge emanating from the house of the Lord. But in order to prepare the way, permit me to make some analogous observations.

Too often have we to lament that the poetry destined to celebrate the nuptial festival is little worthy of Christian marriage: and, in effect, what has the god of the quiver, or Hymen, or Venus, to do with a theme so sacred, or with a union, which is clothed with the august dignity of a sacrament? If the classic writers of paganism, in order to give a charm to their epithalamic strains, enlivened and graced them with the forms and images of their fanciful deities, we can easily excuse and pity them, shrouded as they were in the gloom of error. But that any Christian, of our days, should fashion his eulogy after the model of Latium or of Greece; or what is worse, pandering to the taste of degenerate sensuality, should indulge in epicurean and licentious song, is indeed a subject of indignant and contemptuous regret. This regret is ancient, and has been, a thousand times, repeated; and more than one way has been suggested, by which to get rid of the cause of it.

Some advise that it would be better to dispense altogether with the odes of the muse, and the flowers of Parnassus: and that the most poetic act of life should be passed over, as a common and ordinary occurrence, satisfied with merely a few congratulations that may be offered on the way. But such a proceeding, it seems to me, would not be in keeping with the refinement of our age, or in accordance with the customs of enlightened antiquity. For, without recurring to the writers of Athens or Rome, we find among the people of Israel and all the oriental nations, poetry, coëval with human language, testifying that in all ages, it was customary to celebrate any prosperous event with songs of exultation. And, in truth, so rare, in life, are the occasions in which two families, united in the same object, mingle in the same rejoicing, and festivities, that not to take part in them would be to envy their happiness, or be jealous of their welfare.

Moreover, we cannot tell what good an appropriate ode, or any other poetic strain, may produce in the days of nuptial rejoicings. It is then that the words of another penetrate the heart, and become the seed which will bring forth fruit of honor and praise, in future years. For amidst the pleasant vicissitudes of life,

our hearts are open to feel and profit by
the counsels and gratulations of those who
present themselves before us in the capacity of friends and well-wishers. And
how often have I not seen married persons, when reading over letters and effusions of nuptial congratulation, melt with
the tender reminiscences, and forget for a
time, the troubles and anxieties which
have since thickened around them. And
of such a character should be the tributes
which the present auspicious event calls
forth : tributes not of common-place adu-
lation, not of sickly compliments to "beauteous eyes and golden tresses," but filled
with sentiments which may be comforta-
ble and useful in after times. Some will,
accordingly, dedicate to the bride books
and letters : others will present a golden
coronal of pious counsels and moral precepts, not the less precious because varie-
gated with divers gems and diamonds.

My offering shall be the liturgy—a nosegay gathered in the sanctuary. Human gifts are of little value to the heart that aspires to heaven. If the vision is fixed on the earth, every thing is trifling; if raised to the skies, every thing assumes a character of vastness and grandeur. That among Christians there are some whose thoughts and mode of life are altogether pagan, is a fact which we notice every day. And perhaps the most deplorable instances of it are to be found in the manner in which they receive the sacrament of marriage. Even in the earliest epochs of the world, nothing was held more sacred than conjugal alliances. In a state of nature, the patriarchs, who were not only the rulers of their families, but, likewise, the ministers of religion, never omitted invoking upon their children the benediction of Him in whose hands were the destinies of mankind.

When Abraham bade his servant seek out a spouse for Isaac, he commissioned him with this assurance: "The Lord will send his angel before thee, and thou shalt take from thence a wife for my son."* Actuated by such principles, we are not surprised to see the copious blessings which they brought down upon their children. In their conduct every thing was pure, holy, affectionate, and truly poetical. But, despite the caution of those venerable Fathers, some of the children of the great and powerful of the earth, in selecting their wives, consulted only their inclinations and their passions. Hence the origin of a corrupt race which drew down the vengeance of heaven, in the deluge, in showers of brimstone and fire, and in the awful darkness of idolatry. Their marriages were displeasing to God, and were the sources of innumerable woes.

* Gen. xiv.

Under the Mosaic dispensation, God revived among the people of Israel the memory of their ancient patriarchal traditions: added to matrimony new regulations and ceremonies, and, I may say, prepared it to be elevated to a sacrament in the New Law. And behold among the children of God, we see the archangel Raphael arranging the marriage of Tobias and Sarah: and in the persons of Judith, Esther, and Ruth, we contemplate the beneficent and blessed effects of marriage. When we remark the infinite difference between such nuptials, and those of other nations not governed by the laws of God, but by human legislation, we are compelled to cry out with David: *better to me is the law of thy mouth than thousands of gold and silver!* It is very true that the pagans retained a confused notion of the divine institution of marriage; but the ideas which they entertained of the connubial divinities, tended to the depravation of the spirit and heart, which was not confined to families, but was carried into the very temples of those deities. Few marriages were contracted by the reciprocal sacrifice of bread before the altars and priests of Jove*—most were made by mutual consent before the prætor, which shows that they were regarded as a mere civil contract, that union which could be dissolved at any time.† Hence the tide of libertinism that swept over families and inundated cities, like another deluge. Augustus Cæsar endeavored to restore the bonds of marriage by severe laws, and was, on this account, lauded by the poets, as a god, because: *evaganti fræna licentiæ injecit, amovitque culpas.*‡

He curbed licentiousness and lessened crimes.

* Per confarreationem.
† Per coemptionem.
‡ Horat. lib. 4. Od. xv.

But human laws were insufficient and ineffectual: and where crime abounded, divine grace superabounded. And behold light beams upon the world! behold the *true salt* is scattered over a sterile and contaminated earth! Jesus Christ comes to restore the primitive order of things, and all around is glory unprecedented. Amid the splendor of *material* civilization, the mighty monuments of Jerusalem, Athens, Rome—he introduces a *moral* civilization, and among all men, *of good will*, he proclaims *love*—which was the germ of creation. The love of God, and of man, is the great object of his law, and the *good tidings of great joy*. Nature was to be perfected by grace; and matrimony, brought back to its primitive unity, was raised to the sublime dignity of a sacrament. He restricted it with severe laws, rendered the bond indissoluble, and made it a lily among thorns, and filling it *with grace and truth,* endowed it with abundant benedictions. If any should complain of the severity of the yoke imposed on them by conjugal fidelity, let them but look around, and they will see, at all times, a chosen band of virgins ministering at the altars, and living as though not incumbered with the flesh. The state of virginity is superior to nature, proves how powerfully imperfect man may be strengthened and elevated by grace, and will always be a *light to the world, and salt to the earth,* in as much as it is a perpetual example to the good, and reproof to the slaves of the flesh. Thus did Christ reveal the sublime destiny of human nature, sanctified matrimony, ordaining it not only to propagate this miserable world, but to multiply the number of the elect in heaven.

These and many other similar reflections will present themselves to your mind by a careful study of the Catholic liturgy.

And though the ceremonies are not the same in every country, there is no where any difference in the substance. And to him, who contemplates it with an eye of faith, matrimony, like all the other sacraments, will be an object of sacred reverence.

Its dignity shines forth yet more brilliantly from the holy sacrifice which crowns and seals the conjugal alliance. It is a goodly spectacle to see the tender bride, who, with streaming eyes, making the sacrifice of father, mother, brothers, sisters, unites it with the mysterious sacrifice of Him, who came upon earth not to do his will, but the will of his heavenly Father. Let us view this sight more particularly :

At the *Introit*, the priest repeats the benedictions of the pious Raguel, and the prayer of Tobias and Sarah on the occasion of their marriage. Then he reads the beginning of the hundred and twenty-seventh Psalm, where the royal prophet proclaims the blessings of the man who fears the Lord, and follows his commandments. Thus with the benediction of the ancient pact, he opens the way to the announcement of the *good tidings* that the nuptials are sanctified in the name of the Redeemer.

Having offered a devout prayer to God, through the merits of that holy name, he reads a touching lesson from St. Paul's. *Epistle* to the Ephesians; in which the apostle shows that God is love, and that man, as a dutiful child, should imitate God, and pursue his journey through life under the guidance of charity. The duties of the wife and husband are detailed with such sublimity, that it is easy to perceive, throughout, the Spirit of Wisdom. The intimate union that is formed between man and woman is represented as a sacrament; that is, as a sacred sign of the undying love of Jesus for human nature espoused by himself. And Paul, who, in such glowing terms, commends the state of virginity, evinces no exclusiveness, nor does he become inferior to himself, when there is question of exalting the mysteries of grace which are displayed through the order of nature.

At the *Gospel*, the man-God, Christ himself speaks, and announces the joys of matrimony in the person of Adam and Eve, and promises the same to all true and faithful Christians hereafter. His words are few, but they sparkle like the rays of the sun, and dissipate, like so many clouds, the false notions of men respecting polygamy, divorce, and concubinage. The Redeemer, in the midst of the course of ages, casts around his all-seeing eye, and embracing in his vision, the three grand epochs; the creation, the redemption, and the end of the world, concludes: *Let man not undo the work of God!* and the unanimous expression of gratitude and love bursts from the hearts of all: *Laus Christo!*

The priest then continues, as usual, until he reaches the *Lord's prayer,* when he sends up to the throne of heaven the seven petitions corresponding with the seven wants of the human family, and as peculiarly adapted to the newly married. We need but read this sublime prayer in order to feel its ineffable excellence. The most spiritual doctrine of the creation, and redemption, as there unfolded, in sweet simplicity: and in causing it to be daily repeated by her ministers at the altar, she shows herself to be, in very deed, what she was styled in ancient times, "the tender mother of the faithful."

After the *Ite missa est,* the sacrifice being concluded, a special benediction is given to the married couple, a benediction which will alleviate the common yoke of life, and in the children be the consolation of their fathers; which, in fine, will renovate human kind, and perpetuate the family of Jesus Christ, and cannot, therefore, be too often repeated.

From this brief view of the liturgy, many considerations spring up which give the subject I am treating, an admirable variety! But this is not the place to dilate upon them; I will merely add that the whole of the liturgy accords with the great truths which the venerable philosopher and priest, Antonio Rosmini, has developed in his treatise on divine love. It speaks of the mystic nuptials between the divine and human nature: it represents God as the spouse of our souls: and our souls, in as much as they are raised up to God on the wings of love, are espoused to God. Hence, there has been, throughout the lapse of all ages, but one perpetual spiritual marriage between God and the human soul. The first contract of this marriage was made, in the garden of delights, with the promise of the Redeemer, and continued during all successive ages, in an uninterrupted series of promises and anticipated blessings. The heavenly nuptials were contracted, at length, in the womb of the immaculate Virgin, with a mystery of love that surpasses all understanding, and will be comtemplated with ceaseless ecstasy, in heaven. These nuptials are continued on earth among all who have the spirit of Mary, that is, love of God and of man, and eat of the bread of eternal life at the banquet of the altar. But what will it be, when these nuptials shall be celebrated in Paradise? . . . For the present we may content ourselves with reading, in the Canticle of Canticles, the lively affections with which God deigns to unite himself with the faithful soul. We may partake of the sentiments of the prophet of Patmos, who, seeing the heavens open to his view, and contemplating there the elect, in the bosom of God, exclaimed : I beheld the spouse of God, the church of the elect, clothed with the sun, crowned with stars, having the moon under her feet, and the angels who sang: let us rejoice and give glory to God, because the marriage of the Lamb has come, and blessed are they who are called to the nuptial feast! What an abyss of wonder! Cast your eye upon the earth, and lo! the marvels of nature transport us to the marvels of grace!

I am well aware, that there are men of the world who disregard and, even, condemn things the most worthy of reverence : I, likewise, know, that the two extremes meet in such a manner, that what in the estimation of the pure and believing is an object of holy amazement, is regarded by the irreligious as nothing better than animal sensuality. Still I insist upon what I have already shown, that, if marriages were solemnized with a view to heaven—if the spirit of Christ breathed in the effusions which celebrate the nuptial festivities, the moral lessons derived from them would be sublime indeed. Were they characterized by the enthusiasm and faith with which David sang the nuptials of Solomon,* it would not be surprising, if from the natural love of a husband for his wife, imagination would soar to the infinitely higher love of God for human nature. If in every family could be seen, in miniature, that circle of love with which God surrounds the universe, this world would surely not be deluged with such torrents of tears.

You are convinced, dear madam, of the solid truth of what I have suggested in

* Ps. 44.

this short and unstudied epistle. The church and her ministers must speak nothing but truth, and never should conceal it. Both style marriage a mutual burden, a servitude, a sacrifice: and the more desirous they are to see it blessed by heaven, the greater the duty to insist upon its sanctity and purity. They recommend to the wife inviolable fidelity, gentle virtues, amiable qualities, the love of retirement, silence, simplicity, modesty, and all that can foster harmony, peace, and prosperity in their family. To the husband they recommend, in the government of his house, the example of our heavenly father, and to sweeten his authority with benevolence and love. He should, as far as possible for human nature, present in the domestic sanctuary an image of that immense family which surrounds, in the mansions of love and bliss, the throne of our universal Father.

If there be any who will not receive these wholesome lessons, so much the worse for them. They resist, not the priest, but God. Time will undeceive them, and with bitter remorse, they will regret their folly. How many marriages do we not see, which, contracted in a pagan spirit, end, after a few months of apparent and fictitious contentment, in dissension and divorce, or are a protracted source of contradiction, and misery. Nor is this to be wondered at; for when the married couple do not bring with them to the sacrament the obligations and virtues required, how is it possible for the wife to sustain the character of a "valiant woman," or the husband of a provident father? How can they represent in their offspring the divine Trinity in one love, when they do not take as a model that terrestrial Trinity which shed delight and sanctity in the humble dwelling of Nazareth. Unhappy mortals! they fail in their vocation, which by the operation of love, sweetens the empire of beauty, refines and moralizes man, and enables him to sustain, in a contracted circle, the dominion and exercise of divine charity. The smile of their heavenly Father plays not upon their roof: their house is not the sanctuary of the tranquil virtues, but an emblem of that region of disorder and darkness in which love cannot dwell.

This will not be the case with the virtuous and accomplished pair whose nuptial union fills your generous heart with pleasure. Religion has formed their youth to every virtue: religion will be the ægis and ornament of their future life. Your amiable Julia will cherish, for ever, the beautiful example which you have given her, from her earliest childhood; and will show forth, in herself, that elevation of mind and purity of heart which are so admirable in you. She will carry from her blessed home, deeply inscribed on her heart, the language of Jesus: "let your light shine before men." The distinguished companion of her future days, having proved his many virtues, which his travels over Europe did not, in the least, affect or taint, leaves not a doubt that the piety of his ancestors is deeply rooted in his heart. He possesses an elegant mind: he knows that his beautiful bride forsakes her home for him: and when absent from her loving parents, he will keep before her their image and their benevolence. In these pages I desire to perpetuate, for them, the memory of the vow they have made at the altar. What I have written may serve, perhaps, as an incitement to others: for them, it is, undoubtedly, a panegyric. God grant that their offspring, reading, one day, the merited encomiums of the youthful years of their parents, may have one motive more to style themselves fortunate and favored children.

CARLO FERRERI.

THE NUPTIAL BENEDICTION.

O God of power and light
Who, from the womb of night,
Didst call creation, and its laws approve,
To man, in Eden's shade,
After thine image made
Didst so add woman, in perpetual love,

That from his flesh and bone
Derived, they formed but one,
And thus hast taught us that no power of earth
That sacred tie can sever—
Indissoluble ever,
As when first ordered, at creation's birth:

God, who in after-time,
By mystery sublime,
Didst deign to consecrate this nuptial vow,
That in its sacred tie
Christ's union we descry
With his immaculate spouse, the church below.

THE NUPTIAL BENEDICTION.

O God, by whose decree
Woman was made to be
With man, in sweet companionship, allied;
Whose blessing on the twain
Survived the original stain,
And e'en the deluge graciously defied.

Oh! from thy heavens on high
Look, with a favoring eye,
Upon thy handmaid who implores thy grace:
And may the yoke which here,
She humbly vows to bear,
Be the light yoke of charity and peace.

Chastely in Christ may she
Be wed; and faithfully
May she forever keep before her eyes,
Those models fair and bright,
Which, through the darksome night
Of ages, shine, like beacons, from the skies.

Simple as Rachel be,
Wise as Rebecca she,
Faithful as Sarah, and as full of years:
And may the serpent old
Over her no empire hold—
Whose wiles changed Eden to a vale of tears.

THE NUPTIAL BENEDICTION.

  True to her nuptial bands,
  Faithful to thy commands,
Chaste, modest, strengthened by thy heavenly arm:
  For gravity renowned,
  In Christian doctrine sound,
And venerated for her virtue's charm.

  Arrayed in innocence,
  And void of all offence,
May she behold her numerous offspring rise:
  And having been in life
  A virtuous, Christian wife,
Her's be the rest and glory of the skies.

  And may both, who now
  Their solemn nuptial vow
Before thine altar, Lord, have duly told,
  Hoary with years, through thee,
  Their children's progeny
To the third generation, and the fourth, behold.

THE END.

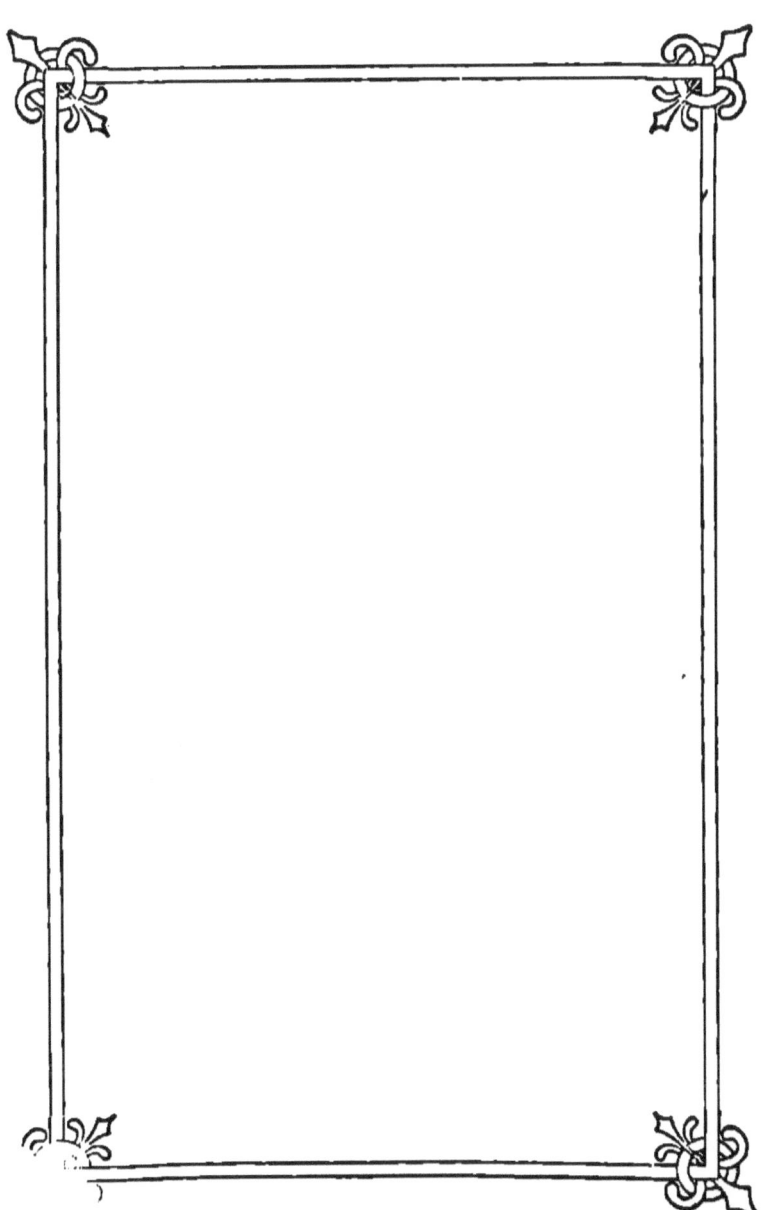

www.ingramcontent.com/pod-product-compliance
Lightning Source LLC
Chambersburg PA
CBHW030735250426
43671CB00035B/434